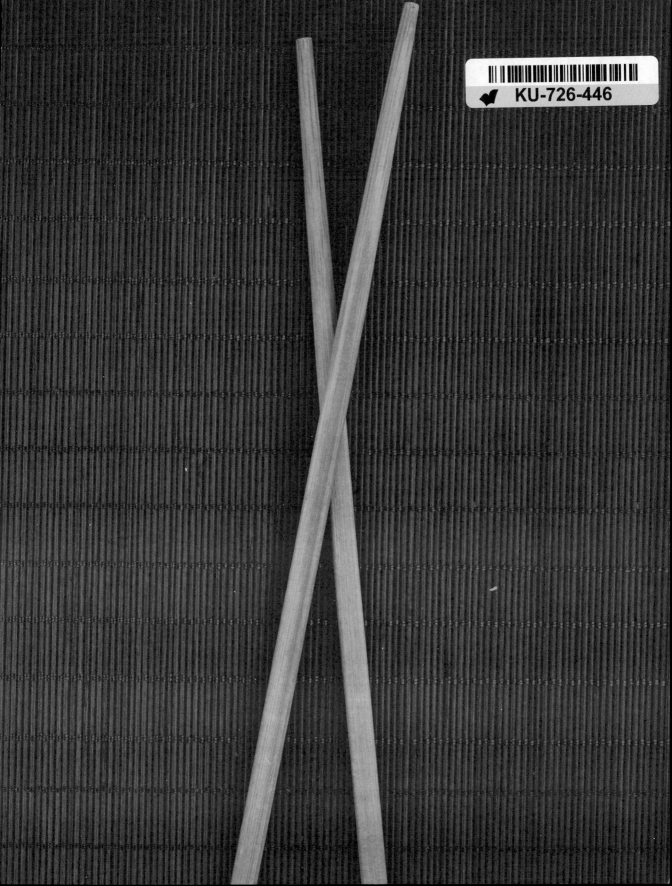

wagamama

feed your soul

wagamama.
feed your soul

fresh + nourishing recipes from the wagamama kitchen

An Hachette UK Company
www.hachette.co.uk

First published in Great Britain in 2019 by
Kyle Books, an imprint of Kyle Cathie Ltd
Carmelite House
50 Victoria Embankment
London EC4Y 0DZ

www.kylebooks.com

ISBN: 978 0 85783 703 5

Publisher: Joanna Copestick
Editorial Director: Judith Hannam
Editorial Assistant: Isabel Gonzalez-Prendergast
Designer: Paul Palmer-Edwards
Photographer: Howard Shooter
Food Stylist: Denise Smart
Prop Stylist: Wei Tang
Production: Gemma John

A Cataloguing in Publication record for this title is
available from the British Library.

Please note, recipes marked vegan or plant-based are only
vegan when using vegan ingredients.

Printed and bound in China

10 9 8 7 6 5 4 3 2 1

I remember standing outside Tokyo's famous Tsukiji fish market and ordering a ramen. The dish was made with only four or five ingredients, including fresh herbs, vegetables and fish. It was exceptional. I was blown away by the flavours, the silky rich broth and the perfectly cooked noodles which had a bit of bite. It was a bowl of simple perfection. This is what made me fall in love with Asian food and that's the spirit we keep alive in wagamama today.

Our hope with this book is that eating the wagamama way is not limited to the times you choose to visit us, but something you can create easily and often in your home. We've shared some of our favourites and made them easy for you to master in your own kitchen. Some recipes will be perfect for relaxed weekends, when you have a little more time on your hands and others can be whipped up in minutes, perfect for a midweek meal. All you need are the fresh ingredients, a healthy appetite and a little pride. The rest is pure enjoyment.

Happy eating.

Steven Mangleshot
Global Executive Chef

feed your soul

From the start, wagamama has believed in the power of 'positive eating' and the idea that our quality of life is determined by the quality of the food we eat. When we feed our bodies what they need – delicious meals that are also nutritionally balanced – we're able to go out and face the day feeling fully alive and energised.

But a full belly alone is not true fulfilment. This book therefore invites you to not only create dishes, but also to take the time to cook, eat and appreciate them. To appreciate and awaken all of the senses, including the sixth sense; your soul. Because your soul gets hungry too.

Feeding your soul sounds impossible, but it's not. Taking a moment to pause and still your thoughts feeds your soul. Mindful practices can help feed your soul, too. This can be practised when you prepare a dish; the time, attention and care you take to both create and consume, regardless of whether it's a feast for friends or just for you. Mindful eating encourages you to appreciate the smaller details; the way the noodles swirl in your ramen broth, how the steam feels on your face, the tingle of chilli on your tongue. It's to be aware of things that mostly go unnoticed or given little thought. Much like the Japanese, wagamama believes food should satisfy the eye as much as it does the stomach.

The recipes that follow are testament to the Japanese philosophy of Kaizen, a philosophy we also share at wagamama and one that has been a guiding principle since we first began. Kaizen means 'continuous improvement' and it encourages us to make small changes, every day, and strive to be better than the day before. In our kitchens, especially when creating new dishes, we challenge ourselves; to find new ingredients, flavours, textures and ways of cooking. Kaizen encourages us to think plant-based, to think sustainably and to think about balance.

The Japanese are renowned for their long life expectancy and Japan is home to the highest number of centurians in the world. Studies suggest the traditional Japenese diet – which is high in protein and vegetables – is the main reason for this longevity of life. Although some of the recipes here are inspired by different parts of Asia, the original inspiration for wagamama came from fast-paced Japanese ramen bars. So, similar to our menu, many dishes in this book have been influenced by Japan. Because of this, we have learnt a lot about Japanese culture, including rituals that we continue to follow and benefit from today. For example, the way ramen should be eaten (which you can read more about in the introduction to our ramen chapter), the importance of variety, and the need to curb intake when you're 80 per cent full (*hara hachi bu*) in order to never feel fatigued.

Most of the recipes have been created for two people, but you have the opportunity to halve, double or even quadruple the ingredients, depending on the occasion. We have purposefully simplified many of the recipes for your convenience but have also included recipes which will teach and enhance your culinary skills, giving you all the necessary knowledge to bring wagamama into your home and feed your soul.

The word wagamama translates as 'naughty child'. But don't mistake us for childish. Rather, we have the characteristics of a wilful and playful child who has a constant need to explore and ask questions.

wagamama began in 1992, in London, a city in which eating-out regularly was a way of life. The decade before had seen a rise in both fast-food outlets and high-end restaurants, but the middle ground was largely unoccupied. When the recession hit, people still wanted to eat out and to experience delicious, real food, but at a price they could afford. wagamama wanted to feed the people and sought to fill that gap.

The vision was to create a new style of noodle bar, one inspired by the fast-paced ramen bars of Japan, but unlike anything you'd find in either London or Tokyo. After all, to be a good student, you shouldn't simply reproduce what you've already been shown, but rather adapt and make it your own. That is the wagamama way.

Right from the start, wagamama challenged restaurant conventions, arguing that eating out should be part of a positive and holistic approach to healthy living. We have pushed boundaries and broken a few 'rules'. Egalitarianism was an unfamiliar concept when we first opened, so to sit right next to an unfamiliar face while eating out was considered unique. Our benches are important to us because we believe that everyone deserves the same experience, no matter who you are. Come to wagamama and you will be treated the same as the person next to you.

We have always been committed to fresh food, it is at the heart of our business. Like our minds, our kitchens are open. We cook with flavour, heat and love.

wagamama came to feed the people, from bowl to soul.

wagamama is all about positive eating, the idea that we feed our soul as well as our body. That's why we use the freshest ingredients, cook our dishes with passion and love, and serve our food the very second it's ready. We want our guests to share our enthusiasm, slurp their noodles, relax in good company and leave feeling happy, nourished and refreshed. Spreading positivity from bowl to soul.

balance

Our inspiration comes from the Japanese and we have learnt from their approach to both eating and living a balanced life. It's an approach that is reflected in our menu and in the recipes you will find in this book, our balanced bowls especially, which are carefully composed of protein and vegetables, much like the traditional Japanese diet.

fresh

Freshness is fundamental to wagamama – fresh ingredients, freshly prepared food and fresh thinking. We are proud of our open kitchens, in which you will never find a microwave or hot lamp. We cook to order, which is why your food arrives at your table as soon as it's ready. Straight from our chef's hands, to yours.

feed your soul

We encourage mindfulness, and there are many simple daily mindful practices and activities to help reduce stress and anxiety, including mindful eating. It's about deliberately noticing what you're eating and showing appreciation for the colours, textures and aromas, by taking time to eat. Taking time allows your body to tell you when you're full. Better yet, try to eat with no distractions like the television or your phone; just you and your bowl.

sustainability

At wagamama we believe in the power of Kaizen; a philosophy which encourages you to make small changes every day, to strive to be better than the day before. It's at the heart of everything we do, and we apply it across every area of our business, including commitment to becoming a more sustainable business. From sourcing our food to the impact we have on the environment. And when it comes to these recipes, we encourage you to use your leftovers, or other vegetables and proteins you might have in your fridge. We also encourage a more plant-based diet, and we hope the recipes in the plant-based power chapter will inspire everyone who reads this.

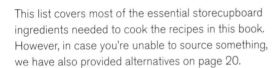

shopping list

This list covers most of the essential storecupboard ingredients needed to cook the recipes in this book. However, in case you're unable to source something, we have also provided alternatives on page 20.

rice vinegar
This is also referred to as rice wine vinegar. It is made from fermented rice and has a slightly sweet flavour that is milder and less acidic than distilled vinegar.

soy sauce
There are two main types; a light version that is most commonly used in cooking or to season food and a dark soy sauce that is stronger in colour and far saltier in taste.

tamari
This is the Japanese version of soy sauce and contains no wheat, which makes it the perfect soy sauce substitute for use in gluten-free dishes.

fish sauce
Or 'nam pla' is a liquid extracted from salted and fermented fish. It is a light golden brown colour and has a pungent, salty taste, which is used to add depth to dishes and enhance the umami flavours.

oyster sauce
This is a thick brown sauce made from oysters cooked down with soy sauce and seasoning.

dashi
A light fish stock made from kombu seaweed and dried bonito flakes.

sweet chilli sauce
A sticky, sweet and subtly spicy sauce that is perfect for serving with spring rolls and tempura. This can be found in most supermarkets.

chilli paste
A simple crushed chilli paste is perfect for adding a spike of heat to any dish or sauce and there are many different kinds. We like Korean 'gochujang', which is sweet, spicy and fermented.

kimchee
A classic Korean side dish which is made by fermenting cabbage and carrots in a flavoursome sauce, pungent with garlic and spice. It is widely available in supermarkets, but we've also created a recipe so you can make your own (see page 161).

bonito flakes
In Japan, dried bonito flakes are also known as katsuo-bushi or katsuobushi. They are flakes of dried, smoked bonito fish (a type of tuna) and can be used to add depth of flavour to stocks and broths, or to finish a dish as a seasoning.

pickled ginger
Widely available and usually served with sushi. We also like to use this fresh, sweet and peppery garnish to finish off many of our stir-fry dishes.

white pepper
Milder than black pepper and is used widely in Asian cooking.

feed your soul | wagamama

chilli oil/chilli flakes
Often used simply to add heat to a sauce or finished dish.

miso paste
A Japanese paste traditionally made from fermented soya beans and some sort of grain, such as rice or barley, and more recently many other ingredient varieties. We mainly use white miso, which is made with rice. White miso has a sweet, light and delicate flavour, which adds a rich umami taste to marinades, sauces and stocks.

sriracha
This South-east Asian hot sauce is made from a paste of chilli peppers, distilled vinegar, garlic, sugar and salt, and is widely available.

crispy fried onions
These bring a lovely crunchy texture and deep savoury flavour to many Asian dishes.

teriyaki sauce
A versatile sauce – it makes a great marinade for grilled meats, oily fish and vegetables, it can be used to finish a dish and also works well as a sweet and salty dipping sauce. We've also created a recipe so you can make your own (see page 148).

kewpie mayonnaise
This Japanese-style mayonnaise is richer than regular mayonnaise as it contains more egg yolk. It also uses mild vegetable oil, rice vinegar instead of white vinegar and additional seasoning, so the taste is full of umami flavours.

panko breadcrumbs
Breadcrumbs with a light, flaky texture. These are generally used in Japanese cooking as a coating for fried or baked food.

coconut milk
This is the liquid that has been extracted from coconut flesh and is used as a base in many of our curry recipes.

shichimi
Sometimes also referred to as 'seven spice pepper', this is a mix of chilli pepper, black pepper, dried orange peel, sesame seeds, poppy seeds, nori seaweed and hemp seeds. It adds a kick of flavour to many noodle stir-fry dishes and is widely available in Asian supermarkets.

sesame oil
Derived from sesame seeds, this oil has a distinct fragrant flavour and complements most Asian dishes.

When designing this book, we wanted to make sure the recipes were as accessible as possible and therefore, while we will always recommend the authentic ingredient first, these substitutes work perfectly well.

edamame
Edamame are young soya beans, most often still in their pod. Due to being picked young, the beans are soft and edible. They can also be found, podded, in the frozen aisles of most large supermarkets.
Ingredient swap | garden peas or broad beans.

mooli
Mooli or 'daikon' is a mild-flavoured radish, native to South-east Asia. In terms of appearance, this vegetable resembles a large, white carrot.
Ingredient swap | salad radish.

menma
Menma is a Japanese condiment made from sun-dried fermented bamboo shoots. We use menma in many of our ramen recipes.
Ingredient swap | tinned bamboo shoots.

shiitake mushrooms
Native to East Asia, these mushrooms (and particularly the dried variety) are rich in flavour and their meaty taste means they work very well in vegetarian stocks and broths. Fresh and dried shiitake mushrooms are available in most large supermarkets.
Ingredient swap | for a fresh shiitake replacement, most mushrooms work well, including chestnut or button. For a dried shiitake replacement, dried porcini will work well.

ponzu
Ponzu is a classic Japanese citrus-based sauce, often used as a marinade or for additional seasoning. It is typically made with rice wine, rice vinegar, bonito fish flakes, seaweed and infused with a Japanese citrus fruit called yuzu.
Ingredient swap | juice of a lemon or lime, with a dash of white vinegar, a tablespoon of soy sauce and a teaspoon of honey. The flavour should be tart so taste and adjust as necessary.

wakame
This edible seaweed originates from Japan. The flavour is subtle with a hint of sweetness.
Ingredient swap | dried nori sheets in supermarkets.

galangal

From the same family as ginger, galangal has a dry, peppery and spicy flavour. It can be found in a paste or dry form in many supermarkets.
Ingredient swap | can be substituted with ginger, but there are flavour differences.

shichimi

This Japanese 'seven-spice pepper', made from a mixture of chilli, black pepper, sesame, hemp and poppy seeds, dried orange peel and nori seaweed, is available at most Asian supermarkets.
Ingredient swap | dried chilli flakes.

miso

Miso is a paste made from fermented soya beans that has a deep, rich umami flavour and can be used to make marinades or add richness to stocks and soups.
Ingredient swap | a mix of light soy, sugar and fish sauce.

dashi

A light fish stock made using kombu seaweed and dried bonito flakes (a smoked tuna-type fish). 'Dashi no moto' is an instant powdered version of dashi and used in many Japanese homes.
Ingredient swap | vegetable stock and a dash of fish sauce.

balanced bowls

These dishes have been created to be a feast for the senses. Visually balanced with vibrant colours, they have multiple textures and bold flavours. Some, like tuna kokoro, are inspired by poké bowls, others by a single Asian ingredient. All of them will ensure that both your body and soul feel truly nourished. These balanced bowls are simple and versatile, so there's one for every occasion.

Packed with protein and fresh, colourful ingredients that contain the vitamins and minerals your body needs, these recipes will help you get your daily intake of fruit and vegetables. They'll also prompt you to explore new ingredients. In Japan, school children are encouraged to eat up to 30 different types of ingredient a day, to ensure they become familiar with variety, and we believe this is a practice we should all adopt, to introduce new flavours and tastes into our everyday life.

Fish plays a big part in this chapter, too. In Japan, fish or seafood in some form are eaten with every meal. In the west, fish is seen as a lighter alternative to red meat, but it's also a great source of protein, omega 3 and nutrients.

Although the dishes in this chapter are generally lighter, the portion size will ensure you don't finish feeling hungry. But if you're looking for a bowl with a little more sustenance, try one that includes grains, such as a donburi.

Rice is a Japanese staple. The Japanese word for it, 'gohan', has two meanings – 'meal' and 'cooked rice' – and prefixes are attached to it to create the words for breakfast (*asagohan*), lunch (*hirugohan*) and dinner (*bangohan*). In other words, in Japan, a meal without rice is not considered a meal.

shiitake mushroom donburi

150g brown rice

2 tablespoons vegetable oil

100g shiitake mushrooms, roughly
   chopped

100g tenderstem broccoli

2 tablespoons Gyoza Sauce
   (*see* page 150)

2 eggs, lightly beaten

2 tablespoons Teriyaki Sauce
   (*see* page 148)

1 large carrot, peeled and grated

2 large handfuls of pea shoots

garnish

2 spring onions, finely sliced

1 large red chilli, deseeded and
   finely sliced

In Japanese, *donburi*, literally translates to 'rice + bowl'. It's a mixture of proteins and vegetables served in a big bowl of rice. This vegetarian version is topped with a shiitake omelette and a sweet teriyaki sauce. It can easily be made vegan by replacing the egg with tofu or vegetables.

Cook the rice following the Perfect Rice cooking instructions on page 180.

Place 1 tablespoon of the oil in a wok over a high heat and stir-fry the mushrooms and broccoli until browned and nicely caramelised. Add 1 tablespoon of the gyoza sauce and stir to coat well.

To make the omelette, pour the remaining tablespoon of oil into the same wok, then reduce the heat and pour in the beaten eggs. Tilt the pan so the egg mixture covers the base and then, as soon as it starts to cook at the edges, shake the pan so any uncooked egg spills into the gaps. When the centre is still slightly runny, fold the omelette in half and slide onto a plate. Set aside.

Divide the rice between 2 serving bowls and coat with the teriyaki sauce.

Slice the omelette into 2.5cm-wide strips and drizzle over the remaining gyoza sauce to taste.

Arrange the omelette strips over the bed of rice and top with the fresh carrot and pea shoots. Scatter over the spring onions and chilli and serve immediately.

feed your soul | **wagamama**

harusame salad

1 skinless chicken breast

175g glass noodles

60g kale, shredded

40g edamame beans, podded

80g mangetout, topped, tailed
and finely sliced

1 carrot, peeled, halved
lengthways and finely sliced

40g canned adzuki beans, drained
and rinsed

60g pea shoots

4 tablespoons Spicy Vinegar
(see page 150), plus extra to
taste

garnish

a few fresh mint sprigs, leaves
picked, to taste

4 tablespoons crispy fried onions

In Japanese, *harusame* literally translates to 'spring rain'. Sounds refreshing, right? But it's also the name of a glass noodle made from beans. This is a light and refreshing salad packed with flavour and crunch. The adzuki beans are a great source of protein and fibre and so provide this salad with plenty of sustenance.

Preheat the oven to 190°C, Gas Mark 5.

Season the chicken breast and place on a baking tray lined with parchment paper and bake for 30 minutes, until cooked through. Set aside to cool, then shred with a fork.

Place the noodles in a heatproof bowl and cover with boiling water. Leave to soak for 10 minutes, then drain and set aside.

Meanwhile, place the kale, edamame beans and mangetout in a pan of boiling water and cook for 3–5 minutes (the vegetables should retain some crunch). Drain and set aside.

Place the noodles, carrot and adzuki beans in a large bowl and toss together with the pea shoots and cooked vegetables.

Add the chicken, drizzle over the spicy vinegar and stir through to coat the ingredients. Add more to taste.

Divide the salad between 2 plates, scatter over the fresh mint and crispy fried onions and serve.

pad thai salad

2 boneless and skinless chicken
   thighs, cut into bite-sized pieces
½ carrot, peeled and grated
1 red onion, finely sliced
2 tablespoons fresh beetroot,
   grated
1 tablespoon vegetable oil
120g mixed salad leaves
5 baby plum tomatoes, halved
150g cooked peeled prawns
50g raw mangetout, finely sliced
100ml Nuoc Cham Dressing
   (*see* page 34)
2 tablespoons crispy fried onions,
   to garnish
2 heaped tablespoons unsalted
   peanuts, roughly chopped, to
   garnish

chicken marinade

2 tablespoons light soy sauce
2.5cm-piece of ginger, peeled and
   grated
1 tablespoon sesame oil
1 garlic clove, crushed
1 teaspoon caster sugar

pickling liquor

5 tablespoons rice wine vinegar
juice of ½ lime
1 tablespoon caster sugar
pinch of sea salt

A lighter colourful version of a classic. Smoked or marinated tofu would also work well as a protein alternative.

Combine the marinade ingredients in a bowl and add the chicken, mixing to coat well. Cover and place in the fridge to marinate for at least 30 minutes.

Place a saucepan over a low heat and add all the pickling liquor ingredients with 3 tablespoons of water. Heat and stir until the sugar and salt have dissolved, then adjust the flavouring to taste. Transfer to a large, heatproof bowl or jar and set aside to cool.

Once cool, add the carrot, red onion and beetroot and stir to mix well, then set aside to pickle for at least 10 minutes, as the longer the pickle is left, the more intense the flavour becomes. When ready to serve, drain the pickling liquid.

Heat the oil in a wok over a medium-high heat. Once hot, add the marinated chicken and stir-fry until browned all over and continue to cook for 2–3 minutes, then set aside.

Place the salad leaves in a large mixing bowl, add the pickled vegetables and stir through with the plum tomatoes, chicken, prawns and mangetout.

Drizzle over the nuoc cham dressing, then divide the salad between 2 serving plates, top with the crispy fried onions, chopped peanuts and serve.

teriyaki mackerel

2 sweet potatoes, peeled and cut
   into wedges
2 tablespoons vegetable oil, plus
   extra for roasting
1 small red onion, finely sliced
100g asparagus spears
120g shiitake mushrooms, roughly
   chopped
100g tenderstem broccoli
80g pak or bok choi, leaves
   separated
1 tablespoon soy sauce
1 tablespoon oyster sauce
1 tablespoon chilli oil
2 mackerel fillets (skin on)
2 tablespoons Teriyaki Sauce
   (*see* page 148)

Mackerel is very popular in Japan as its strong taste is perfectly complemented by robust chilli, garlic and teriyaki flavours. This fish sits on a bed of colourful vegetables and makes the ideal quick and healthy midweek meal. If mackerel isn't for you, try salmon instead as a great alternative.

Preheat the oven to 180°C, Gas Mark 4.

Arrange the sweet potato wedges on a roasting tray and coat lightly with oil. Roast in the oven for 30–45 minutes or until cooked through and slightly caramelised.

Heat 1 tablespoon of the oil in a wok over a medium-high heat and add the onion, asparagus, mushrooms and greens with the sweet potato wedges. Stir-fry for 3–4 minutes or until the mushrooms are cooked through.

Add the soy and oyster sauces and chilli oil and toss to coat, then set aside and keep warm.

Using a sharp knife, score the skin of the mackerel fillets at a 45° angle, being careful not to slice through the flesh. Once scored, pat the skin with kitchen paper to remove any excess moisture.

Heat the remaining vegetable oil in a non-stick frying pan over a high heat, then sear the mackerel, skin-side down, for about 2 minutes, until the skin is crispy and golden.

Carefully turn the fish over and cook, flesh-side down, for a further 30 seconds –1 minute.

Drizzle half the teriyaki sauce over the crispy mackerel skin in the pan.

Divide the stir-fried vegetables between 2 plates. Lay the mackerel on top and drizzle with the remaining teriyaki sauce to serve.

nuoc cham tuna

2 tuna steaks

1 large sweet potato, peeled and
cut into chunks

3 tablespoons vegetable oil

100g quinoa

1 red onion, cut into chunks

1 green pepper, cut into chunks

1 red pepper, cut into chunks

2 heaped tablespoons podded
edamame beans

80g kale, roughly chopped

2 coriander sprigs, leaves picked,
to garnish

marinade

1 tablespoon shichimi

2 tablespoons Gyoza Sauce
(*see* page 150)

nuoc cham dressing

2 tablespoons shichimi

2 tablespoons Spicy Vinegar
(*see* page 150)

Nuoc cham is a Vietnamese-style dressing and has a sweet, sour and spicy flavour. We've used protein-rich tuna in this recipe, which is popular in Japan, and served it on a vibrant base of quinoa and vegetables.

Preheat the oven to 190°C, Gas Mark 5.

Place the tuna in a shallow bowl and cover with the marinade. Cover and set aside in the fridge for at least 30 minutes.

Meanwhile, line a baking tray with foil and arrange the sweet potato chunks on top. Drizzle with 1 tablespoon of the oil and bake for 25–30 minutes until caramelised and soft to cut. Set aside.

Cook the quinoa according to the packet instructions and set aside. Combine the ingredients for the nuoc cham dressing and set aside.

Heat 1 tablespoon of the oil in a wok and sear the marinated tuna for 1–2 minutes on each side until slightly browned. Set aside on a plate.

Add the remaining oil to the same wok and stir-fry the red onion, peppers and edamame beans over a high heat until nicely caramelised.

Add the roasted sweet potato chunks, kale and quinoa and stir-fry until the kale starts to wilt, then stir through 2 tablespoons of the nuoc cham dressing.

Divide the quinoa mixture between 2 plates, place a tuna steak on top and drizzle over the remaining dressing. Finish with a scattering of coriander leaves.

tuna kokoro bowl

150g Thai jasmine rice

2 tablespoons vegetable oil

2 tuna steaks, diced

2 tablespoons shichimi

1 teaspoon sriracha

1 tablespoon mayonnaise

1 egg

2 heaped tablespoons Teriyaki
Sauce (see page 148)

1 medium carrot, peeled and
julienned

4 radishes, finely sliced

½ cucumber, julienned

2 heaped tablespoons podded
edamame beans

2 coriander sprigs, leaves picked,
to garnish

sea salt and freshly ground black
pepper, to taste

In Japanese, *kokoro* has no direct translation but, in essence, it means 'heart, mind and body' so it is the perfect name for a nutrient-rich bowl to feed the body and soul. It is our take on the traditional Hawaiian poké bowl, which serves fresh raw fish with fresh raw vegetables. Prepared simply, taste and texture lead the way.

Cook the rice following the Perfect Rice cooking instructions on page 180.

Heat half the oil in a wok placed over a high heat. Season the tuna then toss gently in the pan to ensure it is seared on all sides, then turn off the heat, add the shichimi and toss again to coat evenly.

In a small bowl, combine the sriracha and mayonnaise, to create sriracha mayonnaise.

Bring a small pan of water to the boil and cook the egg for 3 minutes. Immediately transfer to a bowl of cold water and, once cooled, peel the egg and set aside.

Divide the cooked rice between 2 bowls and, with a fork, fluff up to separate some of the grains. Drizzle over the teriyaki sauce.

Arrange the vegetables, edamame beans and cooked tuna in sections on top of the rice.

Slice the soft-boiled egg in half and place 1 half in the centre of each bowl.

To finish, drizzle over the sriracha mayonnaise, season and garnish with the coriander leaves.

salmon quinoa salad

100g quinoa

1 carrot, peeled and grated

½ cucumber, halved lengthways
   and finely sliced

80g mangetout, finely sliced

100g mixed leaf salad

180g hot smoked salmon flakes

20g mooli, grated

1 red onion, finely sliced

**coconut and horseradish
dressing**

4 tablespoons full-fat coconut milk

2 heaped tablespoons creamed
   horseradish

garnish

1 coriander sprig, leaves picked

1 mild red chilli, finely sliced

**This warm salad is dressed in coconut and horseradish, giving it an
Asian twist and a great spike of flavour to cut through the rich salmon.
The fibre-rich grains and mood-boosting omega 3 fatty acids from the
salmon make this a great midweek meal.**

Cook the quinoa according to the packet instructions and leave to cool.

Meanwhile, make the dressing in a bowl by whisking the coconut milk by hand
until smooth. Add 1 tablespoon of the horseradish and then taste, adding a little
more if you like but note that it's important for the horseradish flavour to come
through as it cuts through the smoky, fatty salmon.

Place the cooled quinoa with the vegetables, salad leaves, flaked salmon, mooli
and onion in a large mixing bowl and add the dressing. Toss together thoroughly
to ensure all the ingredients are coated.

Divide the salad between 2 plates and garnish with fresh coriander and chilli,
to taste.

feed your soul | **wagamama**

seared beef salad

2 x 175g sirloin steaks

1 tablespoon vegetable oil

sea salt and freshly ground black
   pepper, to taste

75g bean sprouts

80g mixed salad leaves

1 red pepper, finely sliced

1 large red onion, finely sliced

½ cucumber, halved lengthways,
   cored and finely sliced

1 carrot, peeled and grated

1 mooli, grated

a few coriander sprigs, leaves
   picked and roughly chopped

2 tablespoons Wagamama
   Dressing (see page 151)

garnish

1 tablespoon mixed sesame seeds

1 tablespoon pickled ginger

A light South-east Asian-inspired salad, vibrant and fresh. Chicken or smoked tofu would work just as well in this salad to replace the beef.

Brush the steaks with the oil, season well and place in a griddle pan set over a high heat. Fry for 2–3 minutes on each side until nicely browned but still a little pink in the centre. Transfer to a warm plate and leave to rest for 5 minutes.

Place the bean sprouts, mixed leaves, red pepper, red onion, cucumber, carrot, mooli and coriander in a large salad bowl and drizzle over the salad dressing. Toss to mix well.

Place a small frying pan over a low-medium heat and toast the sesame seeds for 3–5 minutes, stirring regularly to prevent burning.

Using a sharp knife, slice the beef thinly and then add to the salad bowl.

Divide the salad between 2 serving plates and garnish with the toasted seeds and pickled ginger. Serve immediately.

fresh favourites

A mix of curries, noodles and rice dishes, these recipes are a true reflection of wagamama itself, both past and present. Inspired by Japan, South-east Asia, China and India, each recipe has taken the best of Asian flavours, spices and ingredients, delivering bold vibrancy to your table, ready to awaken your soul.

Some have a western influence too. That's the wagamama way – a beautiful melting pot of the east and west. Firecracker was created to introduce our fans to Korean chilli fire. Pad thai and Katsu curry are both inspired by traditional Asian dishes, which have been adapted to suit a western palate.

Many of the recipes are quick and easy to make, ideal for days when time is limited. Some require a little preparation, but trust us, they're worth the extra effort, especially for weekends at home or when you're impressing friends and family on special occasions. And if you're really wanting to embrace Asian culture, some even make great breakfasts.

okonomiyaki

1 tablespoon vegetable oil

100g green cabbage, finely sliced

2 rashers smoked streaky bacon or
   3 rashers smoked back bacon,
   roughly chopped

pancake batter

100g plain flour

4 large eggs

300ml milk

2 tablespoons vegetable oil

to serve

1–2 tablespoons kewpie
   mayonnaise (*see* page 21)

2 teaspoons Tonkatsu Sauce
   (*see* tip on page 151)

1 nori sheet, torn or dusted

1 tablespoon bonito flakes

2 spring onions, chopped

This versatile pancake is a staple of Japanese cuisine and can be enjoyed as a brunch or as a light evening meal with our raw salad (*see* page 130). This recipe is also great for using up leftovers as almost any ingredient works well in the pancake batter. Chicken, pork and prawns work, as well as every kind of vegetable.

Heat the oil in an 20cm non-stick frying pan and cook the cabbage and bacon, stirring regularly until the fat of the latter has crisped and browned. Set aside.

To make the pancake batter, place the flour in a mixing bowl and slowly whisk in the eggs, milk and 1 tablespoon of the oil.

Stir the cabbage and bacon into the batter, season and mix well.

Heat the remaining oil in a non-stick frying pan, pour in a ladleful or half of the batter mixture and tilt the pan until it coats the surface, then cook for 2 minutes before flipping the pancake and repeating on the other side. When it is cooked, set aside and keep warm while you cook the other pancake.

Serve each pancake with a drizzle of kewpie mayonnaise and tonkatsu sauce and a scattering of nori, bonito flakes and spring onions.

prawn firecracker

120g Thai jasmine rice

1 tablespoon vegetable oil

2.5cm piece of ginger, peeled
and grated

2 garlic cloves, crushed

1 white onion, finely sliced

1 red pepper, finely sliced

1 green pepper, finely sliced

2 spring onions, finely sliced

80g mangetout

150g cooked peeled prawns

1 red chilli, deseeded and
finely sliced

1 dried chilli, finely sliced

100ml Firecracker Sauce
(*see* page 154)

garnish

1 teaspoon shichimi or dried
chilli flakes

1 tablespoon toasted mixed
sesame seeds

1 tablespoon sesame oil

2 spring onions, finely sliced

2 lime wedges

This seriously fiery stir-fry is a wagamama original, inspired by Korea's chilli-rich dishes to bring heat and flavour to our menu. This recipe uses prawns, but chicken or additional vegetables also work well as an alternative.

Cook the rice following the Perfect Rice cooking instructions on page 180.

Heat the oil in a wok or frying pan placed over a medium-high heat and stir-fry the ginger and garlic for 1–2 minutes. Add the vegetables, prawns and both chillies, turn up the heat and stir-fry for 2–3 minutes.

Add the firecracker sauce, turn the heat down to low and simmer for a minute until heated through.

Spoon a portion of rice onto 2 serving plates and top with the prawn and vegetable mixture.

Garnish with the shichimi or dried chilli flakes, toasted sesame seeds, sesame oil and spring onions and serve each portion with a wedge of lime on the side.

kedgeree

200g basmati rice
300ml milk
2 fillets smoked haddock
2 eggs
1 tablespoon vegetable oil
1 leek, finely sliced
1 spring onion, finely sliced
170ml Katsu Curry Sauce
    (*see* page 148)

garnish
parsley sprigs, leaves picked and
    roughly chopped
freshly cracked black pepper,
    to taste

Rice is a staple breakfast ingredient in Asian cooking, and this curried version, inspired by the Indian classic Kedgeree, makes a very satisfying weekend brunch. It uses our mild Katsu Curry Sauce with smoked haddock, but any smoked fish would also work well.

Cook the rice following the Perfect Rice cooking instructions on page 180 and make the curry sauce following the recipe on page 148. Set the sauce to one side.

Place the milk in a large, shallow pan over a medium heat, bring to a simmer, then add the haddock and poach for 4 minutes. When it is just cooked, carefully lift out with a slotted spoon and set aside on a plate. Discard the poaching milk.

Bring a saucepan of water to a simmer and poach the eggs*.

Heat the oil in a wok placed over a medium heat. Once hot, add the leek and spring onion and stir-fry until they begin to caramelise. Take off the heat.

Flake the haddock fillets into the pan and gently stir through the curry sauce.

Divide the rice mixture between 2 serving bowls and top with the poached eggs. Garnish with the parsley and cracked black pepper and serve immediately.

tip | *perfectly poached eggs

Crack each egg into a separate small bowl, ramekin or saucer as this makes it easy to slide the egg into the pan.

Bring a pan of water to a simmer (the water needs to be at least 5cm deep). Add a drop of white wine vinegar to the water, stir to create a gentle whirlpool (this helps the egg white wrap around the yolk) and then slowly tip each egg into the centre.

Cook for 3–4 minutes or until the egg white is set. Lift the poached eggs out with a slotted spoon and drain on kitchen paper.

prawn raisukaree

120g Thai jasmine rice

2 tablespoons vegetable oil

1 red onion, cut into wedges

2 spring onions, chopped

1 red pepper, thickly sliced

1 green pepper, thickly sliced

80g mangetout

1 thumb-size piece of ginger,
    peeled and grated

1 tablespoon garlic paste

150ml vegetable stock

150ml coconut milk

250g cooked peeled prawns

curry paste

1 tablespoon ground cumin

1 tablespoon ground turmeric

2 garlic cloves, roughly chopped

2.5cm piece of ginger, roughly
    chopped

1 lime, juice and zest

1 handful fresh coriander leaves,
    roughly chopped

1 teaspoon caster sugar

2 tablespoons soy sauce

1 stalk lemongrass, stem removed
    and finely sliced

2 spring onions, roughly chopped

1 red chilli, deseeded and finely
    sliced

1 teaspoon fish sauce

pinch of salt

2 tablespoons vegetable oil

garnish

1 large red chilli, deseeded
    and sliced

a few coriander sprigs, leaves
    picked and roughly chopped

2 lime wedges

This is our take on a fragrant Thai green curry. The fresh and light coconut sauce works well with chicken and almost every kind of white fish.

Cook the rice following the Perfect Rice cooking instructions on page 180.

To make the curry paste, heat a wide based pan over a medium-high heat for 5 minutes. Take off the heat and add the cumin and turmeric, then stir well until fragrant, taking care not to burn the spices. Place all the curry paste ingredients into a blender and blitz until smooth.

Heat the oil in a wok placed over a high heat. Once hot, add the red onion, spring onions, peppers, mangetout, ginger, garlic paste and stir-fry for 2–3 minutes until all the ingredients start to caramelise.

Add the curry paste and cook on a medium heat for 10 minutes, then add the vegetable stock and coconut milk. Turn up the heat and bring to the boil. Once boiling, reduce the heat and simmer for 10 minutes.

Add the prawns and cook for 3 minutes to warm through.

Spoon a portion of rice into 2 bowls and ladle over the curry. Garnish with the chilli, coriander and lime wedges.

tip | to make this curry vegetarian, simply replace the fish sauce with light soy sauce and the prawns with more vegetables.

salmon korokke

Makes 6 patties

4 medium-sized potatoes, peeled
and diced

2 steamed salmon fillets

sea salt and white pepper, to taste

4 coriander sprigs, leaves picked
and roughly chopped

plain flour, enough to coat patties

2 tablespoons sriracha

2 tablespoons mayonnaise

2 eggs, lightly beaten

50g panko breadcrumbs

approx. 500ml vegetable oil, for
deep frying

**A 'korokke' is a deep-fried patty made with a soft potato, vegetable, fish
or meat filling and with a crunchy breadcrumb coating. We use salmon,
but any white fish (smoked or unsmoked) also works well. Enjoy these
with our Raw Salad (*see* page 130) or Perfect Rice (*see* page 180) for a
more substantial meal.**

Bring a saucepan of water to the boil and cook the potatoes until tender, then
drain, return them to the pot and mash until smooth.

Flake the steamed salmon (discarding the skin) into the mashed potato.
Season, add the coriander and stir well to combine.

Using your hands, shape the potato and fish mixture into 6 small, flat patties,
pressing firmly so they are compact and hold together well.

Lightly coat each patty with flour and then place in the fridge for at least
30 minutes to firm up.

Meanwhile, combine the sriracha and mayonnaise to make a dipping sauce.

Place the beaten eggs and breadcrumbs in 2 separate shallow dishes.
Dip each patty first in the egg and then in the breadcrumbs, making sure each
is thoroughly coated.

Fill ¾ of a deep saucepan with vegetable oil and place over a medium-high heat.
To test if the oil is hot enough to fry, drop some breadcrumbs into the oil – if they
sink, the oil is not hot enough and, if they quickly burn, then the oil is too hot, but
if they bubble and float to the top, the oil is just right. Deep-fry the korokke in
batches so as not to overcrowd the pan. As the filling is already cooked, they
should only need 2–3 minutes to crisp up and turn golden brown.

Using a slotted spoon, transfer the korokke to a plate lined with kitchen paper,
to soak up any excess oil.

Arrange the korroke on serving plates with a ramekin of sriracha mayonnaise
on the side.

tip | alternatively, these can be shallow-fried and finished off in the oven. To shallow
fry, heat 3–4 tablespoons oil in a large non-stick frying pan over a medium-high heat. When
the oil is hot, add the fish cakes and cook for 5 minutes on each side until golden brown.

surendra's curry

1 tablespoon fennel seeds

30g fresh green jalapeño chillies

1 tablespoon vegetable oil

1 tablespoon red chilli powder

2 teaspoons ground turmeric

2 teaspoons ground cumin

2 teaspoons ginger paste

1 tablespoon garlic paste

2 onions, finely diced

2 skinless chicken breasts, diced

2 heaped teaspoons tamarind
    paste

250ml coconut milk

generous pinch of sea salt

vegetable oil, for deep-frying

garnish (optional)

½ small sweet potato, peeled and
    grated

This fiery curry was created by our Head of Food, Surendra, and takes inspiration from a city in south India called Guntur, which is famous for having the largest chilli farm in Asia and therefore makes great use of red-hot chillies in the local cuisine.

Soak the fennel seeds in water for at least 4 hours or overnight.

Drain the fennel seeds and place in a food processor or blender with the jalapeño chillies. Blitz to a smooth paste.

Heat the oil in a frying pan over a low heat and, once hot, gently cook the chilli powder and ground spices for 3–4 minutes until fragrant, ensuring they don't burn.

Add the ginger and garlic pastes and onions and cook for a further 5 minutes, until the onions turn translucent. Add the jalapeño and fennel paste and continue to cook over a low heat for 10 minutes, stirring occasionally. The oils should release from the paste as a sign that it's ready.

When the oils have released, add the diced chicken and sear all over, then add the tamarind paste and coconut milk and a generous pinch of salt, stir to mix well and simmer for 30 minutes.

Whilst the curry is simmering, prepare the sweet potato garnish, if you like. Fill a medium saucepan halfway with oil and place over a medium-high heat. To test if the oil is hot enough to fry, drop some breadcrumbs into the oil – if they sink, the oil is not hot enough and, if they quickly burn, then the oil is too hot, but if they bubble and float to the top, the oil is just right.

Deep-fry the grated sweet potato in small batches for 2–3 minutes, until crispy and golden. Remove with a slotted spoon and transfer to a plate lined with kitchen paper, to soak up any excess oil.

Divide the curry between 2 bowls and top with the deep-fried sweet potato (if using).

tip | if you can't find fresh jalapeños, use large green chillies.

yaki udon

2 boneless and skinless chicken
thighs
2 tablespoons vegetable oil
450g udon noodles
2 eggs, lightly beaten
20g noyaki chikuwa*
8 cooked peeled prawns
1 leek, finely sliced
1 red pepper, finely sliced
1 green pepper, finely sliced
40g shiitake mushrooms, sliced
80g bean sprouts
1 tablespoon chilli oil, to taste
1 tablespoon light soy sauce
sea salt and white pepper, to taste

garnish
1 tablespoon toasted mixed
sesame seeds
1 tablespoon crispy fried onions
1 tablespoon pickled ginger

Based on an iconic Japanese stir-fry with udon noodles, this simply means 'fried udon' and is a classic wagamama favourite, full of crunchy vegetables and protein.

Season the chicken thighs and heat 1 tablespoon of the oil in a large frying pan or wok over a medium-high heat. Add the chicken and fry until browned all over.

Meanwhile, cook the noodles as per the packet instructions and then place in a large mixing bowl.

Add the eggs, noyaki chikuwa, cooked prawns and chicken to the noodles and stir through so the noodles are thoroughly coated with the egg.

Heat the remaining vegetable oil in a large wok or frying pan over a medium-high heat, add all the vegetables and stir-fry for 2–3 minutes until tender.

Add the noodle mixture to the pan and keep tossing the ingredients to ensure the egg cooks through.

Add the chilli oil and soy sauce, toss the pan again to mix the flavourings through the ingredients, and stir-fry for a further 2 minutes.

Divide the noodles between 2 serving plates and garnish with the toasted sesame seeds, crispy fried onions and pickled ginger.

tip | * noyaki chikuwa is a long-shaped Japanese fish cake. If you can't find any, simply add extra prawns to the dish.

yaki soba

1 skinless chicken breast

1 tablespoon vegetable oil

2.5cm piece of ginger, peeled and grated

1 red pepper, finely sliced

1 onion, finely sliced

4 spring onions, finely sliced

75g bean sprouts

150g cooked peeled prawns

300g soba noodles

2 eggs, lightly beaten

1 tablespoon Worcestershire sauce

1 tablespoon light soy sauce

sea salt and white pepper, to taste

garnish

1 tablespoon toasted mixed sesame seeds

1 heaped tablespoon crispy fried onions

1 tablespoon pickled ginger

This dish, inspired by Japanese street food, has been on the wagamama menu since the day we opened. It's everyone's favourite noodle stir-fry.

Season the chicken with salt and white pepper. Heat the oil over a medium-high heat in a large frying pan or wok and fry the ginger and chicken, until browned all over. Add the pepper, onion, spring onions, bean sprouts and prawns and cook for 2–3 minutes until the vegetables start to brown.

Cook the soba noodles as per the packet instructions.

Place the cooked noodles with the eggs in a large bowl and mix well to ensure the noodles are thoroughly coated. Add the noodles to the pan, tossing quickly to ensure the egg and oil coat the chicken and vegetables thoroughly, then continue to cook for 3–4 minutes, stirring often.

Add the Worcestershire sauce and light soy sauce and toss again, making sure the sauce does not stick to the pan. Add a little more sauce to taste, if necessary.

Divide the mixture between 2 plates and top with the toasted sesame seeds, crispy fried onions and pickled ginger.

chicken and prawn pad thai

2 boneless and skinless chicken
   thighs
2 tablespoons vegetable oil
200g rice noodles
150g cooked peeled prawns
1 leek, finely sliced
1 red onion, finely sliced
2 spring onions, finely sliced
75g bean sprouts
2.5cm piece of ginger, peeled and
   grated
1 garlic clove, crushed
1 red chilli, deseeded and finely
   sliced
pinch of dried chilli flakes
2 eggs, lightly beaten
2 tablespoons Amai Sauce (see
   page 151)
2 tablespoons fish sauce
sea salt and white pepper, to taste

garnish
sprig of coriander, leaves picked
   and roughly chopped
sprig of fresh mint, leaves picked
   and finely sliced
50g unsalted peanuts, roughly
   chopped
2 tablespoons crispy fried onions
2 lime wedges

**A wagamama twist on a classic. Ours uses fresh mint and coriander,
a sweet and salty sauce and a delicious crunchy topping.**

Season the chicken and 1 tablespoon of oil in a large frying pan or wok over a
medium-high heat. Add the chicken and fry until browned all over.

Cook the noodles according to the packet instructions, then drain and set aside.

Place the chicken, prawns, vegetables, ginger, garlic, chilli, chilli flakes and
noodles in a large bowl and mix well.

Heat the remaining oil in a large wok or frying pan over a high heat, tip in the
noodle mixture and stir-fry, ensuring the ingredients move around the pan and
start to cook.

Tip in the eggs and continue to stir-fry until the vegetables start to caramelise
and the egg cooks, about 3–4 minutes.

Add the amai and fish sauces and toss through the ingredients, making sure the
sauce does not stick to the pan. Stir-fry for a further 2 minutes and then remove
from the heat.

Divide between 2 serving plates and scatter with the fresh herbs. Garnish with
the peanuts, crispy fried onions and a wedge of lime and serve immediately.

chicken katsu curry

120g Thai jasmine rice
1 quantity Katsu Curry Sauce (*see* page 148)
2 skinless chicken breasts
50g plain flour
2 eggs, lightly beaten
100g panko breadcrumbs
75ml vegetable oil, for deep-frying

garnish
40g mixed salad leaves
2 tablespoons wagamama Dressing (*see* page 151)
1 tablespoon pickled radish or ginger, or Japanese Pickles (*see* page 158)

Our most iconic and best-loved dish at wagamama, the katsu curry is undoubtably the ultimate Japanese comfort food. We've created this version for you to make at home, which is close to our original, but the only way to experience a wagamama katsu is, of course, in our restaurants.

Cook the rice following the Perfect Rice cooking instructions on page 180.

Meanwhile, make the katsu sauce as per the recipe on page 148.

With a sharp knife, cut each chicken breast almost in half and open it out like a book. Place both between two pieces of clingfilm and bash with a rolling pin to flatten to about 1cm thick.

Place the flour, eggs and breadcrumbs in 3 separate shallow bowls and then dip each chicken breast first in the flour, then the egg and finally the breadcrumbs, ensuring each breast is coated well.

Place the oil in a medium saucepan over a medium-high heat. To test if the oil is hot enough to fry, drop some breadcrumbs into the oil – if they sink, the oil is not hot enough and, if they quickly burn, then the oil is too hot, but if they bubble and float to the top, the oil is just right. Deep-fry 1 coated breast at a time, so as not to overcrowd the pan, for 3–4 minutes on each side then transfer to a plate lined with kitchen paper to soak up any excess oil. Set aside and keep warm.

To serve, spoon a portion of rice onto 2 serving plates. With a sharp knife, slice the deep-fried chicken breasts into strips at an angle and arrange on top of the rice. Ladle the curry sauce over the chicken and rice and place the salad on the side with a drizzle of dressing and a little pickled radish. Serve immediately.

tip | when Steve visited Japan's katsu restaurants, the curries ranged in spiciness from 0–10. Ours is fairly mild so, if you like a little heat, add some chilli powder whilst the sauce is simmering and a splash of sriracha once it is cooked.

teriyaki chicken donburi

200g Thai jasmine rice

2 skinless chicken breasts

4 tablespoons Teriyaki Sauce
(*see* page 148)

2 tablespoons Yakitori Sauce
(*see* page 154)

2 handfuls of pea shoots

1 carrot, peeled and grated

2 spring onions, finely sliced

sea salt and white pepper, to taste

garnish

2 tablespoons toasted mixed
sesame seeds

80g Kimchee (*see* page 161)

Light but filling. Another iconic wagamama dish, this rice bowl is made using the perfect balance of protein, grains and vegetables, and the kimchee gives a great depth of flavour. It tastes best when you mix it all together.

Cook the rice following the Perfect Rice cooking instructions on page 180.

Meanwhile, preheat the oven to 190°C, Gas Mark 5.

Season the chicken breasts and coat with 2 tablespoons of the teriyaki sauce. Place on a baking tray lined with parchment paper and bake for 20–30 minutes until cooked through, then slice into 2.5cm-wide strips. Set aside.

Divide the rice between 2 serving bowls. Arrange the chicken on top and drizzle over the remaining teriyaki sauce with the yakitori sauce.

Add the pea shoots, carrot and spring onions to the bowls and garnish with the toasted sesame seeds and kimchee.

tip | eat donburi the authentic way by stirring all the ingredients together.
Also, why not add more protein with a fried egg. The egg yolk adds a velvety richness when stirred through the dish.

cha han

2 boneless and skinless chicken
   thighs, diced
75g brown rice
2 tablespoons vegetable oil
½ red pepper, chopped
50g closed cup mushrooms,
   sliced
50g shiitake mushrooms, sliced
40g mangetout, sliced
2 spring onions, roughly
   chopped
150g cooked peeled prawns
2 eggs, lightly beaten
2 tablespoons light soy sauce
2 heaped tablespoons Japanese
   Pickles (*see* page 158) or
   pickled ginger, to serve

marinade
2.5cm piece of ginger, peeled
   and grated
4 tablespoons light soy sauce
pinch each of sea salt and
   white pepper

Cha han takes its inspiration from a Chinese street food classic of stir-fried rice. A medley of almost all vegetables and proteins works well in this dish so add your favourites, whatever's in season, or leftovers that need using up in your fridge. Perfectly simple and filling.

Place all the marinade ingredients in a shallow, ovenproof dish, stir well and then add the chicken thighs and coat well in the sauce. Cover, place in the fridge and leave to marinate for at least 30 minutes before cooking.

Cook the rice following the Perfect Rice cooking instructions on page 180.

Heat 1 tablespoon of the oil in a large frying pan or wok over a medium-high heat and fry the chicken until browned all over. Add the remaining oil to the pan and add all the vegetables and the cooked prawns and stir-fry for 1–2 minutes.

Add the eggs to the pan and stir-fry for 2–3 minutes, ensuring all the ingredients are coated as the egg cooks.

Add the cooked rice and soy sauce, turn the heat up to high and stir-fry for a further minute.

Serve with a ramekin of Japanese pickles or pickled ginger on the side.

tonkatsu

180g short grain rice

200g plain flour

1 egg, lightly beaten

100g panko breadcrumbs

2 pork belly slices, sliced into
4 pieces

75ml vegetable oil

4 tablespoons warm Tonkatsu
Sauce (*see* tip on page 151)

wagamama salad

2 portions Raw Salad (*see* page
130) and wagamama Salad
Dressing (*see* page 151)
or a fresh mixed salad and
dressing of your choice

This dish of crispy fried pork belly is served with a sweet sauce, sticky white rice and a fresh, crunchy salad. Japanese comfort food at its best.

Cook the rice following the Perfect Rice cooking instructions on page 180.

Place the flour, egg and breadcrumbs in 3 separate shallow dishes and then dip each pork belly slice first in the flour, then the egg and finally the breadcrumbs, ensuring each slice is coated well.

Heat the oil in a wok placed over a medium-high heat. Once hot, add the breaded pork belly slices and fry for 5–6 minutes on each side until golden brown and crispy. You may need to do this in batches so as not to overcrowd the wok.

Transfer the fried pork to a plate lined with kitchen paper to soak up any excess oil.

Prepare the salad and drizzle over the dressing.

Divide the rice between 2 plates, arrange the pork belly slices on top and drizzle over the warm tonkatsu sauce. Place the salad on the side and serve.

teriyaki lamb

2 lamb leg steaks or 6 cutlets

2 tablespoons Teriyaki Sauce (see page 148), plus extra to serve

pinch of chilli flakes

200g soba noodles

2 tablespoons vegetable oil

60g mangetout, finely sliced

100g asparagus, finely sliced

100g mixed mushrooms

handful of kale

2 tablespoons light soy sauce

pea, herb and wasabi dressing

4 tablespoons garden peas

4 tablespoons rapeseed oil

pinch of chilli flakes

juice of ½ lime

1 tablespoon soy sauce

1 teaspoon wasabi paste

a few coriander sprigs, leaves picked

a few sprigs Thai basil, leaves picked

garnish

a few coriander sprigs, leaves picked and roughly chopped

1 fresh red chilli, deseeded and finely sliced

Steve's favourite dish. The pea, herb and wasabi dressing adds freshness to the dish and complements the lamb. We use lamb leg steaks in our wagamama recipe, but lamb cutlets are widely used in Japan and work well in this recipe.

Place the lamb in a shallow dish, coat with the teriyaki sauce and chilli flakes, cover and leave to marinate overnight in the fridge, or for at least an hour.

To make the dressing, add the peas to a small pan with water. Bring to a boil until cooked, then drain and set to one side. Add the peas with all the remaining dressing ingredients to a blender and blitz until it forms a smooth paste. If too thick, add more oil to loosen. Taste and add more soy or wasabi as needed. Set to one side.

Bring a pot of salted water to the boil and cook the noodles as per the packet instructions.

Heat the oil in a frying pan or wok over a medium-high heat and cook the lamb for approximately 3 minutes on each side (for medium-rare). Lift out onto a plate and set aside to rest.

Add the noodles, mangetout, asparagus, mushrooms and kale to the pan and stir-fry for 3–4 minutes or until heated through. Add the light soy sauce and cook for a further minute.

Tip the noodle mixture into a large bowl and toss through the pea, herb and wasabi dressing.

Using a sharp knife and a chopping board, cut the lamb into 2.5cm-thick slices, discarding the bone in the middle.

Divide the noodle mixture between 2 serving plates, arrange the lamb on top and drizzle over the extra teriyaki sauce. Garnish with the coriander leaves and chilli.

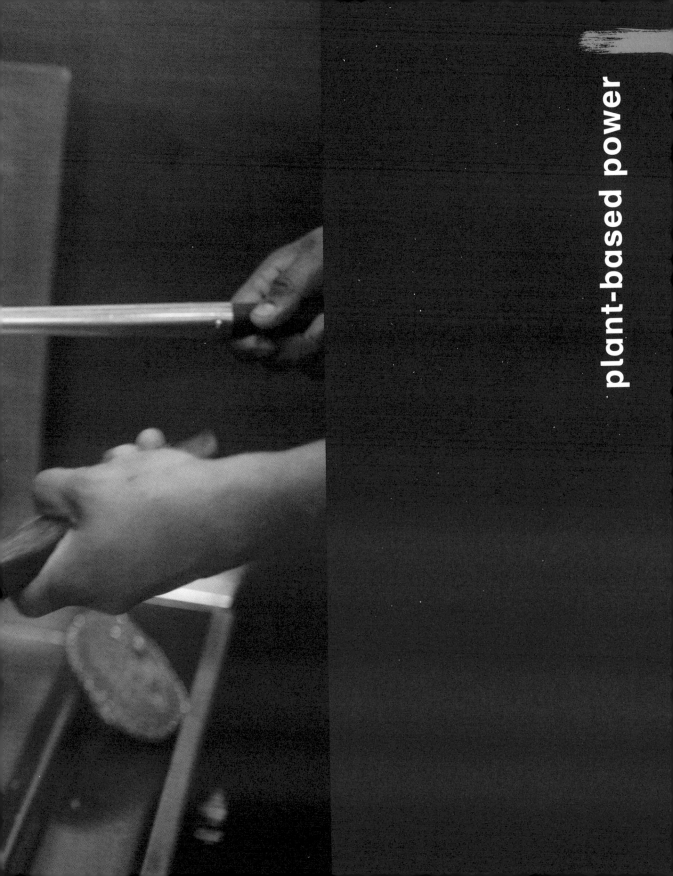

plant-based power

True to the Japanese diet, which contains very little animal fat or dairy, many of our dishes have always been vegetarian and vegan. Plant-based food and a reduction of meat is becoming increasingly mainstream, and with this in mind we have been on our own plant-based journey, the kaizen way. We've continued to develop and expand our vegan horizons, which has meant re-working a few wagamama classics to be plant-based. As we explored possibilities, we created dishes specifically with the vegan palate in mind. At wagamama, a lifestyle choice which is meat-free doesn't have to mean taste-free. The recipes in this chapter are flavourful and filling. The flavours are bold and the colours bright. Perfect mindful meals.

A few of the recipes celebrate a single ingredient, such as the king oyster mushroom or asparagus. These make impressive side dishes or delicious toppings for rice or grains, paired with vegan kimchee. Others, such as itame or samla curry, use tofu as the protein source. Made from the humble soy bean, tofu is the most consumed protein in Japan. Soy is nutritiously superior compared to other vegetable proteins, and is also consumed as soy sauce, miso and soya milk.

You'll also find our juices in this chapter. wagamama has served fresh juices since our doors first opened because we believe in raw power, a power that can only be found in uncooked fruits and vegetables. They are the most effective way of consuming vitamins, minerals and enzymes to help boost your body's immune system.

coconut porridge

50g rolled oats
300g coconut yogurt

mango, chilli and passionfruit sauce
3 tablespoons maple syrup
juice of ½ lime
50g frozen or fresh mango, diced,
   plus extra to serve
1 passion fruit, flesh scooped
2.5cm ginger, peeled and finely
   sliced
pinch of chilli flakes

A nourishing and fulfilling breakfast packed with tropical flavours of coconut, mango and ginger. Switch in your favourite fruits and seeds to top the creamy oats

To make the sauce, add the maple syrup, 3 tablespoons of water and the lime juice to a small saucepan over a medium-low heat. Add the mango and passion fruit flesh, ginger and chilli flakes, stir and cook gently for 2–3 minutes until you reach a syrupy consistency. Add more maple syrup and water to taste.

To make the porridge, add 200ml water into a small non-stick pan, stir in the porridge oats and cook over a low heat until bubbling and thickened.

Stir through the coconut yogurt and top with the fruit sauce and fresh mango.

vegetable tempura

80g tenderstem broccoli

approx. 500ml vegetable oil, for
  deep-frying

1 red pepper, cut into 2.5cm-wide
  strips

80g asparagus

10g wakame, to garnish (optional)

tempura batter

75g cornflour

35g plain flour

2 teaspoons baking powder

80ml iced soda water

sea salt and white pepper, to taste

dipping sauce

2 tablespoons Amai Sauce (*see*
  page 151)

1 tablespoon light soy sauce

1 tablespoon malt vinegar

1 teaspoon caster sugar

pinch of chilli flakes

generous pinch of salt

**Japanese tempura is a light and crispy batter which makes these
vegetables a savoury addiction. Serve as a side together with a simple
grilled protein.**

First make the batter. Place the two flours and baking powder in a bowl and stir
through enough iced soda water to make the batter the consistency of single
cream (it should coat your finger). Season with a pinch of salt and white pepper.

Bring a pot of salted water to the boil and blanch the broccoli for 3 minutes, then
strain and plunge into a large bowl of iced water. Cool for 30 seconds, then strain
and set aside.

To make the dipping sauce, add the ingredients to a small pot and bring to a
simmer over a low heat. Stir until the sugar and salt have dissolved. Once the
liquid starts to reduce, mix well and take off the heat.

Heat the oil in a large wok or deep fat fryer and wait for it to reach 190°C
(see tip below).

Dip each of the prepared vegetables in the batter until thoroughly coated and then
lower into the hot oil. Work in batches to ensure you don't overcrowd the pan.

Fry for 2 minutes or until golden brown, then remove with a slotted spoon and
transfer to a plate lined with kitchen paper to soak up any excess oil.

Divide the tempura between 2 small serving plates and garnish with the wakame.

Serve with the dipping sauce on the side.

tip if you don't have a kitchen thermometer, dip the handle of a wooden spoon or a
chopstick into the oil. If the oil starts to bubble gently, the oil is ready for frying. If the
oil bubbles too vigorously, it means it is too hot, so lower the heat slightly.

wok-fried greens

100g tenderstem broccoli

2 tablespoons vegetable oil

200g pak or bok choi, leaves
picked and tough part of stalks
removed

1 garlic clove, finely sliced

1 tablespoon light soy sauce

1 tablespoon vegetarian oyster
sauce or dark soy sauce

pinch of salt

This dish takes inspiration from the traditional Thai vegetable stir-fry 'morning glory'. Smoky and salty, it makes a great side to any simple grilled protein, or use to top rice with some charred tofu on the side.

Bring a pot of salted water to the boil and blanch the broccoli for 3 minutes, then strain and plunge into a large bowl of iced water. Cool for 30 seconds, then strain and set aside.

Heat half the oil in a wok over a medium-high heat and stir-fry the broccoli, pak or bok choi and garlic until the pak or bok choi starts to wilt.

Add the light soy and oyster sauces, mix well and reduce over a high heat for 3–5 minutes, stirring occasionally. Serve.

bang bang cauliflower

4 tablespoons vegetable oil

1 head of cauliflower, broken into
small florets

1 red onion, finely sliced

2 spring onions, finely sliced

1 quantity Firecracker Sauce (*see*
page 154)

garnish

2.5cm piece of ginger, peeled and
finely sliced

a few coriander sprigs, leaves
picked

**'Bang Bang Chicken' is traditionally served in China as a street food snack
and is so-called because of the method of tenderising the chicken with
a hammer before it's coated in a spicy sauce and fried. We've created a
plant-based alternative. The flavour of the sauce is sweet, salty, smoky
and spicy and makes a perfect side dish.**

Place half the oil in a wok over a high heat and stir-fry the cauliflower for 5–8
minutes until browned.

Add the remaining oil to the pan and stir-fry the red onion and spring onions until
slightly caramelised.

Stir in the firecracker sauce and simmer to heat through.

Divide the cauliflower between 2 serving bowls and top with the fresh ginger
and coriander.

stir-fried king oyster mushrooms

1 tablespoon vegetable oil

200g king oyster mushrooms, thickly sliced lengthways

2 tablespoons Gyoza Sauce (see page 150)

to serve

2 teaspoons Amai Sauce (see page 151), to serve

1 small red chilli, deseeded and finely sliced

a few coriander sprigs, leaves picked and roughly chopped

Oyster mushrooms are very popular in Asian cooking as they're very good at absorbing flavour. We've used king oyster mushrooms here because they're deliciously meaty and easy to handle. They would work well as part of a plant-based 'donburi' rice bowl, together with Thai jasmine rice and fresh crunchy vegetables.

Heat the oil in a non-stick frying pan over a high heat and, once hot, fry the king oyster mushrooms until browned.

Add 1 tablespoon of the gyoza sauce and cook for 2–3 minutes until the sauce has been absorbed, then turn the mushrooms, add the remaining sauce and cook until it has been absorbed again.

Serve with a drizzle of amai sauce and garnish with the fresh chilli and coriander.

warm chilli tofu salad

2–3 tablespoons vegetable oil

1 aubergine, halved lengthways and finely sliced

100g tofu or firm tofu, drained and cubed (*see* instructions on page 180)

20g cornflour

125g asparagus, finely sliced

1 red pepper, finely sliced

100g tenderstem broccoli, sliced

100g mangetout

1 red onion, finely sliced

1 tablespoon sweet chilli sauce

2 tablespoons Korean barbecue sauce

2 Baby Gem lettuces, leaves removed, hearts reserved and finely sliced

1 tablespoon wagamama Dressing (*see* page 151)

garnish

1 red chilli, deseeded and finely sliced

2 spring onions, finely sliced

20g unsalted cashew nuts

This sweet and smoky salad takes inspiration from Thai flavours, with a delicious crunch of cashew nuts. Use the fresh lettuce leaves to scoop up the tofu and vegetables.

Heat 1 tablespoon of the vegetable oil in a frying pan or wok set over a medium-high heat and fry the aubergine until golden brown on each side. Transfer to a plate and set aside.

Prepare the tofu as per the instructions for Perfectly Pressed Tofu on page 180, then place in a shallow bowl and generously coat each piece with cornflour.

Heat another tablespoon of oil in the frying pan or wok and fry the tofu on all sides until crispy and golden. Transfer to a plate and set aside.

Add the asparagus, red pepper, broccoli, mangetout and red onion to the wok and stir-fry over a medium heat for 6–7 minutes, tossing occasionally and adding a further splash of oil if necessary.

Take the pan off the heat, add the aubergine and tofu and stir through the sweet chilli and barbecue sauces.

Divide the lettuce leaves and hearts between 2 serving plates and drizzle over the salad dressing. Arrange the tofu and stir-fried vegetables on top and garnish with the chilli, spring onions and cashew nuts.

yasai itame

150g firm or extra firm tofu,
   drained and cubed (*see*
   instructions on page 180)

30g cornflour

1 tablespoon vegetable oil

100g pak or bok choi, leaves
   picked and tough parts of
   stalk removed

2 small red onions, finely sliced

1 red pepper, sliced

2 spring onions, finely sliced

60g shiitake mushrooms, sliced

100g bean sprouts

1 garlic clove, crushed

1 red chilli, deseeded and finely
   sliced

250ml coconut milk

250ml Vegetable Stock
   (*see* page 163)

300g rice noodles

coconut ginger curry paste

2 garlic cloves

2.5cm piece of ginger, peeled

2.5cm piece galangal, peeled

2 lemongrass sticks, outer leaves
   removed

150ml hot water

3 coriander sprigs, leaves picked

1 teaspoon caster sugar

sea salt and white pepper

garnish

2 coriander sprigs, leaves picked

2 lime wedges

This fragrant coconut and lemongrass broth is filled with rice noodles and fresh, colourful vegetables. It is versatile, so use up any leftover vegetables you have in your fridge.

First, make the curry paste. Place all the ingredients in a blender and blitz until smooth.

Prepare the tofu as per the instructions for Perfectly Pressed Tofu on page 180, then place in a shallow bowl and generously coat each piece with cornflour.

Heat the oil in a frying pan or wok placed over a medium-high heat and fry the tofu on all sides until crispy and golden. Transfer to a plate and set aside. Replace the oil, if needed, or reheat the oil in the pan. Add the curry paste and stir-fry for up to 3–4 minutes.

Add the vegetables, garlic and chilli to the pan (with more oil if necessary) and stir-fry until the red onion and pepper become lightly caramelised. Add the tofu, coconut milk and stock and simmer for 5–10 minutes.

Meanwhile, bring a pot of water to the boil and cook the rice noodles according to the packet instructions, then drain and set aside.

Divide the noodles between 2 deep serving bowls. Ladle the broth over the top with the vegetables and tofu and garnish with the coriander leaves and a wedge of lime.

kare burosu

300g udon noodles
150g firm tofu, drained and cubed
    (*see* instructions on 180)
30g cornflour
500ml Vegetable Stock
    (*see* page 163)
1 tablespoon mild curry paste
2 tablespoons vegetable oil
30g shichimi
250g mixed mushrooms (we love
    a mix of oyster, shiitake, closed
    cup and chestnut), finely sliced
2 tablespoons Gyoza Sauce
    (*see* page 150)
2 handfuls of pea shoots
1 carrot, peeled and grated

garnish
1 red chilli, deseeded and finely
    sliced
2 coriander sprigs, leaves picked
    and roughly chopped

Created and named by us, it literally translates as 'curry broth'. The curry-infused broth provides a rich depth of warming flavours and pairs perfectly with the spicy and crispy tofu.

Bring a pot of water to the boil and cook the udon noodles according to the packet instructions, then drain and set aside.

Prepare the tofu as per the instructions for Perfectly Pressed Tofu on page 180, then place in a shallow bowl and generously coat each piece with cornflour.

Place the stock and curry paste in a large saucepan over a medium-high heat. Bring to the boil and then reduce to a simmer.

Heat the oil in a frying pan or wok and fry the tofu on all sides until crispy and golden. Transfer to a plate and coat well with the shichimi. Set aside.

Add the sliced mushroom mix to the wok and stir-fry for 2 minutes, then add the gyoza sauce and continue to stir-fry for a further 2 minutes until heated through.

While the mushrooms are cooking, add the udon noodles to the hot stock to revive and heat through.

Divide the stock and noodles between 2 serving bowls and scatter over the pea shoots and grated carrot.

Arrange the fried shichimi tofu and mushrooms on top and garnish with the chilli and coriander.

yasai samla curry

200g firm tofu, drained and cubed
 (*see* page 180)
30g cornflour
250g short grain rice
2 tablespoons vegetable oil
300ml coconut milk
2 teaspoons tamarind paste
pinch of sea salt
1 green pepper, sliced
1 red pepper, sliced
100g shiitake mushrooms, sliced
50g baby plum tomatoes, halved

curry paste

1 teaspoon turmeric
1 teaspoon chilli powder
1 teaspoon ground coriander
2 onions, finely chopped
2 shallots, finely chopped
3 heaped tablespoons desiccated
 coconut
2.5cm piece of galangal, peeled
 and grated
1 lemongrass stalk, pale part only
2.5cm piece of ginger, peeled and
 grated
2 garlic cloves, finely chopped

garnish

1 chilli, deseeded and sliced
2 spring onions, chopped
small handful of coriander, leaves
 picked and roughly chopped

This subtly spiced Cambodian-inspired curry is rich with coconut and fragrant lemongrass. The sauce is versatile, so add your favourite vegetables and proteins to make it your own.

Prepare the tofu as per the instructions for Perfectly Pressed Tofu on page 180, then place in a shallow bowl and generously coat each piece with cornflour.

Cook the rice following the Perfect Rice cooking instructions on page 180.

Heat 1 tablespoon of oil in a frying pan or wok placed over a medium-high heat and fry the tofu on all sides until crispy and golden. Transfer to a plate lined with kitchen paper to soak up any excess oil. Set aside.

Make the curry paste by placing the spices, onions, shallots, desiccated coconut, galangal, lemongrass, ginger and garlic in a food processor. Blitz to a smooth paste.

Place the remaining oil in a wok over a medium heat and cook the curry paste for about 10 minutes or until the oil starts to separate from the paste.

Add the coconut milk and tamarind paste to the wok with a pinch of salt and stir to combine.

Add the green and red peppers, mushrooms, tomatoes and tofu and turn up the heat to bring to the boil. Reduce to a simmer and cook for 20–30 minutes.

Divide the curry between 2 bowls and top with the chilli, spring onions and coriander. Serve with a bowl of the rice on the side.

tip | for presentation, serve the rice in a neat, rounded dome in the centre of your serving dish. Simply pack the rice into a lightly oiled small bowl or rounded cup and then turn out onto a plate to serve.

age dashi

2 tablespoons cornflour

200g firm tofu, drained and sliced into 4 pieces (*see* instructions on page 180)

2 tablespoons vegetable oil

60ml Vegetable Stock (*see* page 163)

1 teaspoon light soy sauce

1 teaspoon vegetarian oyster sauce or dark soy sauce

garnish

1 spring onion, finely sliced

5g wakame

2.5cm piece of ginger, peeled and finely sliced

This is another of Steve's favourites. It is a Japanese-inspired dish that typically uses dashi – a stock made from bonito fish flakes and kelp seaweed. However, we have created a plant-based version that is just as rich in umami flavours.

Place the cornflour in a shallow bowl and generously coat each piece of tofu.

Heat the oil in a non-stick frying pan over a medium-high heat and fry the tofu on all sides until crispy and golden. Set aside.

Heat through the vegetable stock on a low heat. Add the soy and oyster sauces to 2 small serving bowls, add the vegetable stock and mix well.

Divide the tofu between the 2 bowls and top with the spring onion, wakame and ginger. Serve immediately.

tip to enrichen and add more umami flavour to the broth, dissolve a teaspoon of white miso paste in the stock.

mushroom ramen

1 tablespoon vegetable oil

100g shiitake mushrooms, roughly
   chopped

100g button mushrooms, roughly
   chopped

1 tablespoon light soy sauce

1 tablespoon vegetarian oyster
   sauce or dark soy sauce

200g udon noodles

500ml Vegetable Stock
   (*see* page 163)

stock base

2 teaspoons sriracha

2 teaspoons Amai Sauce
   (*see* page 151)

1 teaspoon light soy sauce

1 teaspoon malt vinegar

pinch of sugar

pinch of salt

garnish

2 small handfuls of pea shoots

1 small handful of mint

1 small handful of coriander leaves

1 red chilli, deseeded and
   finely sliced

A light take on a Vietnamese pho packed with earthy, smoky mushrooms and fresh fragrant herbs. For more protein, this dish works well with the addition of tofu.

Heat the oil in a frying pan or wok, add the chopped mushroom mix and stir-fry for a minute. Add the light soy and vegetarian oyster sauces and continue to stir-fry for a further 2 minutes until cooked through.

Meanwhile, bring a saucepan of water to the boil and cook the noodles according to the packet instructions.

Place the stock base ingredients in a small saucepan over a low heat and bring to a simmer. Stir until the sugar and salt have dissolved. Once the liquid starts to reduce, add the vegetable stock and mix well.

Divide the drained noodles between 2 serving bowls and pour over the stock. Top with the cooked mushrooms and finish with a scattering of pea shoots, mint, coriander and chilli.

juices + smoothies

positive power juice

makes 1 juice

2 apples, roughly chopped
40g spinach
100g fresh pineapple,
   roughly chopped
¼ cucumber, sliced
juice of ½ lime

This vitamin-packed green juice is a great way to kickstart your day. If you don't have a juicer, replace the apples with 1 banana and 50ml fresh orange or apple juice.

Place all the ingredients in a juicer or blender and blitz until smooth.

Pour through a strainer, if necessary, and serve immediately.

tropical summer juice

makes 1 juice

1 mango, peeled, stoned and
   roughly chopped
1 apple, roughly chopped
100g fresh pineapple, peeled and
   roughly chopped
juice of ¼ lime

Filled with the tropical flavours of mango and pineapple, this juice is like sunshine in a glass. To make it into a smoothie, simply replace the apple with a banana and add 50ml coconut milk or coconut water.

Place all the ingredients in a juicer or blender and blitz until smooth.

Pour through a strainer, if necessary, and serve immediately.

spiced berry boost smoothie

makes 1 smoothie

100g frozen blueberries
150g fresh lychees, peeled
   and stoned
juice of ½ lime
2.5cm piece of ginger, peeled
   and grated
200ml coconut milk (or vegan milk
   of your choice) or coconut water

This creamy coconut smoothie also has a kick from the ginger and lime and works well with almost any berry. Add chia seeds for extra protein.

Place all the ingredients in a juicer or blender and blitz until smooth.

Pour through a strainer, if necessary, and serve immediately.

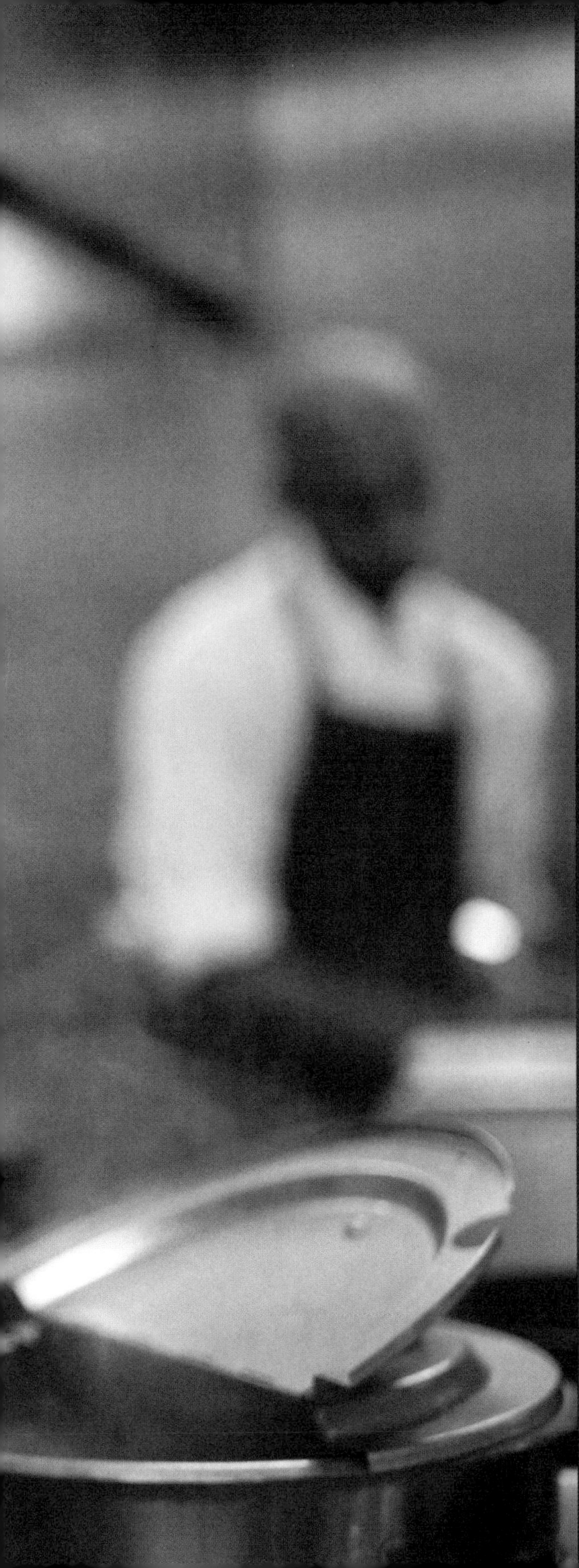

soulful ramen

Ramen. It's where it all began for us. Our inspiration came from the fast-paced ramen bars in the back-streets of Tokyo. How quickly the bowls were consumed, but also how masterfully they were put together.

There are many Japanese traditions and rituals when it comes to eating ramen, which we still respect today. It's about eating it mindfully. Paying close attention to each component; firstly, to observe the finished dish, paying close attention to the glistening jewels of chilli oil or the swirling noodles and floating spring onions or herbs. Allow the steam to warm your face and inhale the aromas slowly. Eat the noodles first, but don't bite them; that's bad luck! Instead, slurp, as noisily as possible, and smack your lips to show true appreciation.

Noodles are the heart of the ramen, but the soul of the bowl is the broth. This takes time to prepare, but the ramen itself can be served in minutes, making it a renowned 'fast-food' in Japan. Noodles were invented by the peasants of China, but it wasn't long before they were being sold on the streets and feeding the emperor. They soon made their way to Japan, where they developed two types of noodle; one made with buckwheat, now known as soba noodle, and one much fatter and made with wheat, known as udon.

Ramen will offer your body everything it needs. Carbohydrate from the noodles, a healthful broth, protein and vitamin-rich vegetables. All of this feeds your body, but most importantly, it's a soulful bowlful. A moment to lose yourself deep in steam and feed your soul.

kimchee prawn ramen

10 raw king prawns, shelled with
  tail on
1 tablespoon vegetable oil
100g soba noodles
600ml Vegetable Stock
  (*see* page 163 or use a
  good-quality stock cube)
2 tablespoons fish sauce
4 tablespoons Chilli Katsu Sauce
  (*see* page 155)
100g bean sprouts
2 spring onions, finely sliced
2 tablespoons Kimchee
  (*see* page 161)
2 coriander sprigs, leaves picked
1 lime, quartered

prawn marinade
2 tablespoons Chilli Katsu Sauce
  (*see* page 155)
1 tablespoon rice wine vinegar

Kimchee adds a lovely depth of flavour to ramen, bringing spice with a touch of sweetness and a crunchy texture which complements the soft noodles and prawns in this dish.

Place the marinade ingredients in a shallow bowl and stir to mix, then add the prawns and turn over until thoroughly coated. Set aside to marinate in the fridge for at least 30 minutes.

Heat the oil in a wok over a medium heat and, when hot, stir-fry the prawns until pink and cooked through. Once cooked, set aside.

Bring a pan of salted water to the boil and cook the noodles according to the packet instructions, then set aside.

Add the vegetable stock to the wok with the fish sauce and chilli katsu sauce and stir to heat through.

Divide the stock mixture between 2 bowls and stir through the noodles.

Arrange the bean sprouts, spring onions, kimchee, prawns and coriander on top of the noodles and finish with a squeeze of lime.

miso cod ramen

4 cod fillets
3 tablespoons vegetable oil
200g soba noodles
200g pak or bok choi
500ml Vegetable Stock (*see*
   page 163 or use a good-quality
   stock cube)
2 teaspoons light soy sauce
1 teaspoon oyster sauce
1 tablespoon fish sauce

cod marinade

1 tablespoon white miso paste
2 teaspoons mirin
1 tablespoon soy sauce
2.5cm piece of ginger, peeled
   and grated
1 tablespoon sesame oil

garnish

2 spring onions, finely sliced
12 pieces menma
1 tablespoon chilli oil, to taste

Fish is a staple of the Japanese diet and this light, savoury ramen allows the cod to be the star of the dish. Inspired by miso black cod, the marinade is packed with delicious umami flavour.

Place the marinade ingredients in a wide, shallow bowl and stir to combine. Add the cod fillets and coat well, then cover and leave to marinate in the fridge for at least 30 minutes.

Heat 2 tablespoons of the oil in a frying pan or wok over a medium heat until hot and place the cod fillets, skin-side down, into the pan. Pan-fry the fish for 2–3 minutes until the skin is golden brown, then turn and cook for a further 2–3 minutes on the other side. Transfer the fish to a plate and set aside.

Bring a pan of salted water to the boil and cook the noodles according to the packet instructions, then set aside.

Add the remaining oil to the wok and stir-fry the pak or bok choi until it starts to wilt. Add the vegetable stock to the wok with the soy, oyster and fish sauces and stir to heat through.

Divide the noodles between 2 serving bowls and add the broth. Top with the pak choi and cod and garnish with the spring onions, menma and a drizzle of chilli oil, to taste.

chicken ramen

2 skinless chicken breasts
1 tablespoon vegetable oil
200g soba noodles
2 tablespoons shirodashi sauce
500ml Chicken Stock
  (*see* page 165)
pinch each of sea salt and
  white pepper
light soy sauce, to taste

garnish
40g pea shoots
10 pieces menma
2 spring onions, finely sliced

You can't beat a classic light and fresh bowl of comforting ramen, our Japanese version of chicken soup for the soul. For extra flavour, add some light soy sauce and chilli oil.

Preheat the oven to 190°C, Gas Mark 5.

Rub the chicken all over with oil, season and place on a baking sheet in the oven for 20–30 minutes or until cooked through.

Bring a pot of salted water to the boil and cook the noodles according to the packet instructions, then drain and set aside.

Combine the shirodashi sauce and chicken stock in a saucepan, mix well and bring to a simmer over a low heat.

With a sharp knife, slice the cooked chicken breasts at an angle.

Divide the stock between 2 serving bowls and stir in the noodles. Arrange the chicken on top and garnish with the pea shoots, menma and spring onions. Add a splash of light soy sauce to taste, if you like. Serve immediately.

shirodashi ramen

150g pork belly slices
2 tablespoons Korean barbecue
   sauce
200g ramen noodles
2 tablespoons shirodashi sauce
600ml Chicken Stock
   (*see* page 165)
sea salt and white pepper, to taste

garnish
20g pea shoots
1 spring onion, finely sliced
10 pieces of menma
10g wakame or nori
1 medium-boiled egg, peeled and
   halved

This soulful ramen of slow-cooked pork belly in a rich savoury broth makes a deliciously warming meal, perfect for those cold, crisp nights.

Preheat the oven to 160°C, Gas Mark 3.

Pat dry the pork belly with kitchen paper and season.

Place the pork on a baking tray lined with parchment paper and cover with half the Korean barbecue sauce. Tightly cover with foil and roast for 1½ hours, until the meat is completely tender.

Remove the foil and turn the grill to its highest setting. Grill the meat for 3–4 minutes, turning it halfway and brushing with the barbecue sauce on the tray, until the sauce becomes thick and sticky and the slices have caramelised and charred.

Transfer the pork to a chopping board and, with a sharp knife, slice into thin strips. Arrange on a plate and cover with the remaining barbecue sauce, then set aside.

Bring a pan of salted water to the boil and cook the noodles according to the packet instructions, then set aside.

Combine the shirodashi sauce with the chicken stock in a saucepan and whisk well to ensure both liquids have combined. Place over a medium heat and bring to a simmer.

Divide the noodles between 2 serving bowls. Ladle over the hot broth and arrange the pork slices on top. Garnish with the pea shoots, spring onion, menma, wakame or nori and egg halves. Serve immediately.

tantanmen beef brisket ramen

150g beef brisket

200g soba noodles

1 tablespoon vegetable oil

1 tablespoon Korean barbecue
sauce

1 tablespoon Stock Base
(*see* page 166)

500ml Chicken Stock
(*see* page 165)

beef marinade

2.5cm piece of fresh ginger,
crushed

2 garlic cloves, crushed

1 tablespoon vegetable oil

200ml Vegetable Stock (*see*
page 163)

generous pinch of salt and
black pepper

garnish

2 heaped tablespoons Kimchee
(*see* page 161)

2 spring onions, finely sliced

12 pieces menma

2 coriander sprigs, leaves picked

1 medium-boiled egg, peeled
and halved

2 teaspoons chilli oil, to taste

Based on a traditional tantanmen, which is a Japanese adaptation of the Chinese 'dan dan noodles', this ramen is typically spicy and packed with flavour. Our version uses slow-cooked beef brisket, which is rich and flavoursome.

Preheat the oven to 140°C, Gas Mark 1.

Rub the beef with the ginger and garlic cloves, and season with salt and pepper, then cover and set aside for at least 30 minutes in the fridge.

Place a heavy bottomed pan on a medium heat and, once hot, add the cooking oil. Place the beef in the pan, fat side down, and sear all sides for 3–5 minutes until browned on all sides.

Once sealed, place the beef in an ovenproof dish with the vegetable stock and cook for 4–5 hours or until the meat falls apart easily. Check the beef every hour and baste with the cooking liquid. Shred the meat, using 2 forks, and set aside, reserving the cooking liquid.

Bring a pan of salted water to the boil and cook the soba noodles according to the packet instructions, then set aside.

Heat the oil in a wok over a medium heat. Once hot, add the shredded beef with the Korean barbecue sauce, stir to coat and stir-fry for 2–3 minutes until hot. Set aside.

Add the stock base to a saucepan with the chicken stock, whisk well to ensure the broth and stock base have combined. If you'd like to add more depth of flavour, add spoonfuls of the cooking liquid from the beef brisket until the desired flavour is reached.

Divide the noodles between 2 serving bowls. Ladle over the hot broth and arrange the beef on top. Garnish with the kimchee, spring onions, menma, coriander and egg halves and drizzle over the chilli oil, to taste.

short rib ramen

4 tablespoons light soy sauce

350g beef short rib or 2 beef short ribs

1 tablespoon vegetable oil

1 small sweet potato, sliced into ribbons*

handful of mangetout, finely sliced

1 small red onion, finely sliced

1 large carrot, peeled and julienned or grated

500ml Chicken Stock (*see* page 165)

pinch of dried chilli flakes

200g soba noodles

generous pinch of sea salt

handful of pea shoots

A western twist on a traditional ramen. We like to use short rib because of its tender and rich flavour, which comes from the bone and infuses the broth.

Preheat the oven to 130°C, Gas Mark 1.

Place the soy sauce, 1 tablespoon of water and a generous pinch of salt in an ovenproof dish, add the meat to coat and stir. Cover with foil and roast for 5 hours or until the meat is tender, basting with the light soy sauce and roasting juices every hour.

Once the meat is cooked, keep it covered and set aside.

Heat the oil in a wok placed over a high heat and stir-fry the sweet potato, mangetout, red onion and carrot for 2–3 minutes, then set aside.

Heat the chicken stock in a saucepan with a pinch of chilli flakes and bring to a simmer.

Bring a pan of salted water to the boil and cook the noodles according to the packet instructions, then set aside.

Divide the broth between 2 serving bowls, stir through the noodles and top with the pea shoots. Create a nest with the stir-fried vegetables and lay the beef on top. Serve immediately.

tip | *use a vegetable peeler to create ribbons. If you can't find beef short rib, use a piece of braising steak instead.

sides + small plates

This chapter is here to encourage you to experiment and to give you a chance to get your hands a bit messy. Some take a little practice and time, such as gyoza and hirata steamed buns, and some are quick and easy, like our summer rolls, filled with vibrant colours and fresh ingredients. But whichever you choose to make, they will all result in you serving up some impressive side dishes to delight your guests.

If you want to make your big bowls even better, find a side that perfectly pairs with your main. Balance the flavours and create a harmony; sweetness with saltiness. Chilli heat and creamy coconut. Our favourite pairing is gyoza and ramen. Gyoza are small crescent-shaped dumplings originating from China, much like the noodle. Each is filled with vegetables or meats, usually dipped in soy, vinegar or oil, but also just as satisfying when dipped in a steaming bowl of ramen broth.

Some of our sides are perfect for picnics or lunch, as the flavours intensify after they cool off. If you're really up for a challenge, line your table with small plates and share with friends. This is egalitarianism at its best.

chilli squid

1 squid, body only, about 200g
50g cornflour
150ml vegetable oil
1 teaspoon shichimi
generous pinch of salt, plus extra
   to taste
1 tablespoon Spicy Vinegar (*see*
   page 150)

Another wagamama favourite, this is our take on salt and pepper squid, using spicy Japanese shichimi as seasoning. Serve with our dipping sauce, which cuts through the heat. Be warned, this dish is hugely addictive!

First prepare the squid. Rinse it under cold water and drain on a plate lined with kitchen paper. Ensure it is thoroughly dry before frying for good, crispy results.

Transfer the squid to a chopping board and slice it open down the middle so you are left with a rectangular shape. Remove any thin or excess skin to ensure the surface is smooth and soft.

Using a sharp knife, lightly score the inside of the squid in a small grid or diamond pattern, then slice into 2cm-wide pieces.

Place the cornflour in a shallow bowl and dip the squid pieces in the cornflour, ensuring they are all thoroughly coated.

Heat the oil in a deep frying pan or wok. Once the oil is hot, add the squid pieces and fry for approximately 2 minutes until pale golden. Do not fry for too long as they will become tough and chewy, work in batches if necessary.

Using a slotted spoon, transfer to a plate lined with kitchen paper to drain off any excess oil.

Mix the shichimi and salt together in a bowl. Add the fried squid and toss to coat.

Serve immediately with spicy vinegar on the side for dipping.

salmon tataki

1 tablespoon vegetable oil

1 salmon fillet

1 tablespoon shichimi

1 tablespoon kewpie mayonnaise

½ fresh chilli, deseeded and finely
    sliced, to garnish

pickled mooli

5 tablespoons rice wine vinegar

1 tablespoon caster sugar

juice of ½ lime

pinch of sea salt

30g mooli, grated

citrus ponzu dressing

1–2 teaspooons ponzu

1 teaspoon mirin

½ teaspoon rice wine vinegar

1 tablespoon tamari

juice of ½ lime

½ teaspoon chilli oil

½ teaspoon sesame oil

Tataki is widely popular in Japan and makes a lovely light but impressive dinner party side or starter dish. Tuna would also work well with the zesty ponzu dressing.

Place the oil in a frying pan or wok over a medium-high heat and, once hot, sear the salmon on each side for 2–3 minutes. Remove from the heat and transfer to a plate. Dust over the shichimi and cover. Place in the fridge until chilled.

To make the pickled mooli, whisk together the vinegar, sugar, lime juice and sea salt with 3 tablespoons of water in a deep bowl. Add the mooli and stir to coat in the dressing. Leave to pickle while you make the rest of the dish.

To make the citrus ponzu dressing, combine all dressing ingredients in a small dish and set to one side.

Take the chilled salmon and, using a very sharp knife, slice the fillet into 6 even slices.

Place the pickled mooli in the centre of a small serving plate and lay the salmon slices on top. Put a spot of kewpie mayonnaise on the side and garnish with the chilli slices before serving.

lollipop prawn kushiyaki

12 large raw king prawns, peeled
   and deveined
1 tablespoon vegetable oil
1 lime, cut in half

marinade
1 teaspoon sugar
1 teaspoon water
1 tablespoon malt vinegar
1 tablespoon light soy sauce
pinch of salt
1 coriander sprig, leaves picked
   and finely chopped
½ red chilli, deseeded and
   finely chopped
1 garlic clove, crushed

'Kushi' is a type of skewer and kushiyaki means 'grilled skewer'. These garlicky grilled prawns are a great addition to a stir-fry or salad. The caramelised lime adds zest and sweetness, and they are just as good cold as they are warm. You will need 6 small wooden skewers.

Place all the marinade ingredients in a large, shallow bowl. Reserving 1 tablespoon of the marinade to use later, place the prawns in the marinade and stir to coat well. Cover and set aside to marinate for up to 30 minutes.

Once marinated, thread 2 prawns on each skewer.

Heat the oil in a non-stick frying pan or griddle. Place the lime, cut-side down, in the pan, add the skewered prawns and cook for 3–4 minutes, turning halfway through, until caramelised (and cooked through).

Arrange the skewers on a serving plate with the glazed lime and drizzle with the reserved marinade.

tip | if using wooden skewers, soak them in water for at least 10 minutes prior to cooking with them as this will prevent the wood from burning.

gyoza

These pockets of filled pastry are versatile and delicious. When you have a little time on your hands, make your own gyoza skins (*see page 182*). Alternatively, these can be found ready-made in most Asian supermarkets.

chicken gyoza

makes 30 gyoza

1 skinless chicken breast, roughly chopped

2 spring onions, roughly chopped

2 garlic cloves, crushed

2.5cm piece of ginger, grated

2–3 coriander sprigs, leaves picked

2 tablespoons light soy sauce

generous pinch of pepper

Place all the ingredients in a food processor and pulse until the mixture becomes almost smooth. If you don't own a food processor, use minced chicken and combine the ingredients thoroughly using your hands.

Fill the gyoza and cook, following the method on page 182.

yasai gyoza

makes 30 gyoza

100g shiitake mushrooms, finely chopped

40g kale, shredded and tough stalks removed

1 large sweet potato, peeled, chopped and steamed until soft

1 red chilli, finely chopped

2 garlic cloves, crushed

2.5cm piece of ginger, grated

2–3 coriander sprigs, leaves picked and finely chopped

1 heaped teaspoon white miso paste

1 tablespoon light soy sauce

generous pinch of pepper

Place all the ingredients in a large bowl and, using your hands, mix well to combine thoroughly.

Fill the gyoza and cook, following the method on page 182.

prawn gyoza

makes 30 gyoza

400g cooked and peeled prawns, finely chopped

3 spring onions, very finely chopped

50g tinned bamboo shoots, finely chopped

1 lemongrass stalk, tough part removed and finely chopped

2.5cm piece of ginger, grated

2 garlic cloves, crushed

1 tablespoon light soy sauce

2 tablespoons fish sauce

1 tablespoon vegetable oil

small handful of chives, finely chopped

small handful of parsley, leaves picked and finely chopped

generous pinch of white pepper

Place all the ingredients in a bowl and, using your hands, mix well, making sure the mixture is evenly combined. Fill and cook the gyoza following the steps on page 182.

raw salad

1 carrot, peeled and grated

1 small red onion, finely sliced

30g mooli, grated

100g mixed salad leaves

40g pea shoots

20g podded edamame beans

5 baby plum tomatoes, halved

30g wakame

60ml wagamama Dressing (*see* page 151)

2 tablespoons crispy fried onions, to garnish

pickling liquor

5 tablespoons rice wine vinegar

juice of ½ lime

1 tablespoon caster sugar

pinch of sea salt

This salad may look simple but the wagamama dressing is full of flavour and it makes a great accompaniment to other small plates if you fancy a light meal.

Place all the pickling liquor ingredients in a saucepan with 3 tablespoons of water over a low heat and stir until the sugar and salt have dissolved. Transfer to a heatproof bowl and set aside to cool.

Once the liquid has cooled, add the carrot, red onion and mooli and set aside to pickle while you make the rest of the salad.

Combine the salad leaves, pea shoots, edamame beans, tomatoes and wakame in a large mixing bowl and toss through the dressing.

Serve in 2 small salad bowls and garnish with the crispy fried onions and pickled vegetables.

vg

grilled asparagus

125g asparagus spears
pinch of dried chilli flakes
pinch of garlic powder
1 teaspoon vegetable oil
juice of ½ lime (optional)
1–2 tablespoons Yakitori Sauce
   (*see* page 154)
sea salt
1 tablespoon toasted mixed
   sesame seeds

Simple and delicious. This side dish works well with almost any dish either as a side or simply paired with your favourite grilled protein.

Bring a salted pan of water to the boil and blanch the asparagus for 1–2 minutes, then strain and transfer to a plate.

Season the asparagus with a pinch each of salt, chilli flakes and garlic powder.

Lightly oil a griddle pan over a medium heat and then sear the asparagus all over for 1–2 minutes.

Arrange the asparagus on a serving plate, squeeze over the lime juice and drizzle over the yakitori sauce. Finish with a scattering of toasted sesame seeds and serve.

makes 8–10 rolls

2 skinless chicken breasts

1 heaped tablespoon Thai Green
  Curry Paste (see page 155)

70g vermicelli noodles

Spicy Vinegar (see page 150), for
  dipping

8–10 rice paper wrappers*

4 mint sprigs, leaves picked and
  chopped

4 coriander sprigs, leaves picked
  and chopped

1 carrot, peeled and julienned
  or grated

chicken summer rolls

**These Vietnamese-inspired summer rolls are packed with crunchy
vegetables and marinated chicken and, served with a gyoza dipping
sauce, they make a great light lunch or an impressive dinner party dish.**

Preheat the oven to 190°C, Gas Mark 5.

Coat the chicken breasts in the curry paste, season and place on a baking tray
lined with parchment paper, then cook in the oven for 20–30 minutes or until
cooked through.

Meanwhile, cook the noodles as per the packet instructions and set aside.

Using 2 forks, shred the chicken and then set aside.

Prepare the spicy vinegar for dipping and set aside.

134

½ cucumber, deseeded and cut
    into matchsticks
20g kale, finely shredded
sea salt and white pepper, to taste

*rice paper wrappers can be found
in most big supermarkets or
specialist Asian shops

To assemble the summer rolls, fill a bowl about a quarter full with warm water and soak each rice paper wrapper for 15–20 seconds, or until softened, then transfer to a plate or work surface and blot with kitchen paper to remove excess water.

Take a rice paper wrapper and, in the centre, place a small amount of noodles, shredded chicken, fresh herbs and vegetables.

Fold the edge closest to you up over the filling, using your fingers to carefully tuck the filling in. Next, fold in the 2 sides over the top to secure the filling and then carefully and tightly roll up each summer roll. Repeat with the remaining rice paper wrappers and filling ingredients to make 8–10 rolls.

Arrange the summer rolls, seam-side down, on a plate or board and serve with a bowl of the spicy vinegar on the side for dipping. To impress guests, these look great when sliced on a diagonal to reveal the colourful ingredients inside.

feed your soul | **wagamama**

tori kara age

250g boneless chicken thighs,
cut into 5cm pieces

1 egg, lightly beaten

½ teaspoon dried thyme

½ teaspoon dried oregano

2 teaspoons cornflour

approx. 500ml vegetable oil, for
deep-frying

sea salt and white pepper, to taste

2 tablespoons Gyoza Sauce
(*see* page 150), for dipping

1 lime, cut into wedges, to serve

chicken marinade

2.5cm piece of ginger, peeled
and grated

1 small garlic clove, crushed

50ml light soy sauce

50ml mirin

1 tablespoon oyster sauce

pinch of sugar

Japanese fried chicken is packed full of flavour. It's best to use chicken thighs as the meat stays deliciously tender under the crunchy coating. Enjoy either as a side dish or with rice and Asian slaw as a main meal.

Place all the marinade ingredients in a mixing bowl and stir through the chicken pieces to coat. Cover and leave to marinate in the fridge for at least 30 minutes, or ideally overnight.

In a bowl, place the egg with the dried herbs, salt and pepper and cornflour and mix until smooth. Add the marinated chicken and coat with the mixture.

Fill a medium saucepan halfway with oil and place over a medium-high heat. To test if the oil is hot enough to fry, drop some breadcrumbs into the oil – if they sink, the oil is not hot enough and, if they quickly burn, then the oil is too hot, but if they bubble and float to the top, the oil is just right. Working in batches so as not to overcrowd the pot, deep-fry the chicken pieces for 5 minutes until golden brown. Use tongs or chopsticks to separate any chicken that sticks together in the oil.

Transfer the chicken to a plate lined with kitchen paper to soak up any excess oil. Set aside and keep warm, while you cook the rest.

Serve with the gyoza dipping sauce and a fresh wedge of lime or 2 on the side.

tip | these also work really well with sriracha mayonnaise as a dipping sauce. Simply combine 1 tablespoon sriracha with 1 tablespoon mayonnaise.

tebasaki chicken wings

12 chicken wings

2 tablespoons sunflower oil

pinch of sea salt

½ teaspoon freshly ground black
pepper

Korean barbecue sauce

2 teaspoons sesame oil

1 garlic clove, crushed

2.5cm piece of ginger, peeled and
finely sliced

75ml gochujang

75ml Teriyaki Sauce
(*see* page 148)

2 teaspoons caster sugar

pinch of white pepper

1 teaspoon dark soy sauce

1 teaspoon light soy sauce

garnish

1 tablespoon toasted mixed
sesame seeds

2 spring onions, finely sliced
at an angle

**Our take on Japanese chicken wings, using a sweet and spicy Korean
barbecue sauce. Enjoy as a side dish with a fresh Asian slaw or salad.**

Preheat the oven to 180°C, Gas Mark 4.

Place the chicken wings on a baking tray lined with parchment paper and season
with the oil, salt and pepper. Bake for 30 minutes.

While the wings are cooking, make the barbecue sauce. Add the sesame oil to
a small saucepan over a medium heat. Once hot, add the garlic and ginger and
stir-fry for 2–3 minutes until fragrant. Add the remaining sauce ingredients and
simmer for 2 minutes. Remove from the heat and set aside.

Drain off any excess oil from the tray and increase the oven temperature to
200°C, Gas Mark 6. Coat the wings in the barbecue sauce, reserving some for
later, and return to the oven for a further 20–30 minutes, until sticky and brown.

Transfer the chicken to a serving plate, drizzle over a little more barbecue sauce
if necessary and garnish with the toasted sesame seeds and spring onions.

tip | this barbecue sauce also works well with pork ribs.

duck lettuce wraps

2 duck legs, skin removed
2 tablespoons tamari
1 tablespoon vegetable oil
6 Baby Gem lettuce leaves
½ cucumber, finely sliced
sea salt and white pepper, to taste
2 spring onions, finely sliced,
    to garnish

These Chinese-inspired wraps are crunchy and packed with savoury flavour. They make a great light meal.

Preheat the oven to 180°C, Gas Mark 4.

Season the duck legs on both sides, then place on a wire rack set over a roasting tray and cook in the oven for approximately 1 hour and 10 minutes.

Remove the duck from the oven and coat with 1 tablespoon tamari, then reduce the temperature to 160°C, Gas Mark 3 and return to the oven for a further 10 minutes. Once cooked, shred the meat with a fork and set aside.

Heat the oil in a frying pan or wok over a medium-high heat, add the shredded duck and remaining tamari and stir-fry for 3–4 minutes.

Divide the lettuce leaves between 2 serving plates and arrange the cucumber and shredded duck on top. Garnish with the spring onions and serve.

beef yakitori

225g sirloin steak, sliced into
   2.5cm cubes
3 tablespoons Yakitori sauce
   (*see* page 154)
1 tablespoon vegetable oil
1 spring onion, sliced into 2.5cm
   pieces

Yakitori, meaning 'grilled chicken', are a typical Japanese street food served on skewers. We've made ours with steak for more depth, but chicken or salmon works just as well.

Place the beef in a bowl and coat with 2 tablespoons of the yakitori sauce. If you have time, cover and leave to marinate in the fridge for at least 30 minutes.

Heat the oil in a large frying pan over a medium-high heat. When hot, sear the beef for 2 minutes on each side, basting continually with the sauce and ensuring the meat is evenly cooked. Set aside to rest for 5 minutes.

Once rested, thread the beef onto a skewer with a piece of spring onion between each piece of meat.

Drizzle the skewers with the remaining yakitori sauce and arrange on a plate to serve.

hirata bun fillings

Small, pillow-like buns filled with proteins, pickles and flavour-packed sauces. Soft, fluffy and perfect for sharing. If you have time and really want to impress your friends, why not make your own buns (see page 174).

mixed mushroom + panko aubergine

makes 6 buns

1 egg, lightly beaten
2 heaped tablespoons panko
    breadcrumbs
½ small aubergine, sliced into
    1cm-thick rounds
2 tablespoons vegetable oil
30g mixed mushrooms, sliced
1 tablespoon light soy sauce
6 Hirata (steamed) Buns
    (see page 174)

garnish

1 tablespoon kewpie mayonnaise
1 coriander sprig, leaves picked
    (optional)

Place the egg and breadcrumbs in 2 separate shallow bowls and dip the aubergine slices first into the egg and then into the breadcrumbs, ensuring each slice is coated well.

Heat the oil in a wok over a medium-high heat and, once hot, shallow-fry the aubergine slices until crisp and golden on both sides. Transfer to a plate lined with kitchen paper to soak up any excess oil and set aside.

Drain the oil from the wok and then fry the mixed mushrooms, without stirring, for 4–5 minutes. Add the soy sauce and stir to coat, then stir-fry for a further 5 minutes.

Take a hot steamed bun, prise it apart gently and fill with some fried aubergine and some mushrooms.

Add a little kewpie mayonnaise and garnish with fresh coriander, if you like.

Repeat with the remaining buns and serve warm.

sticky duck

makes 6 buns

2 duck legs, skin removed
3 tablespoons hoisin sauce, plus
    extra to serve
1 tablespoon vegetable oil
6 Hirata (steamed) Buns
    (see page 172)
½ cucumber, peeled into ribbons
sea salt and freshly ground black
    pepper, to taste

garnish

½ red chilli, deseeded and finely
    sliced
2 spring onions, finely sliced
1 coriander sprig, leaves picked

Preheat the oven to 190°C, Gas Mark 5.

Season the duck legs with salt and pepper on both sides, then arrange on a wire rack set over a roasting tray and cook in the oven for approximately 1 hour and 10 minutes.

Remove the duck from the oven and reduce the temperature to 160°C, Gas Mark 3. Coat the duck with 2 tablespoons of the hoisin sauce, then return to the oven for a further 10 minutes. Once cooked, shred the meat with a fork and set aside.

Heat the oil in a frying pan or wok, add the shredded duck and remaining hoisin sauce and stir-fry for 3–4 minutes.

Take a hot steamed bun, prise it apart gently and fill with a cucumber ribbon and a portion of duck. Top with a little chilli, spring onion and coriander and more hoisin sauce, to taste.

Repeat with the remaining buns and serve warm.

feed your soul | wagamama

sauces + marinades

sauces

Many of these sauces can be found in supermarkets but some, like katsu curry sauce, are signature to wagamama and are best when made from scratch. These sauces, dressings and marinades elevate the dishes in this book. They add depth, cut through rich proteins, or simply add the finishing touch to a noodle or rice-based dish. They are the element that give many of these recipes the wagamama finish.

teriyaki sauce [1]

makes 125ml

4 tablespoons light soy sauce
110g caster sugar
1 tablespoon dark soy sauce
2 tablespoons sake

This sauce works as a great marinade for grilled meats, oily fish and vegetables. It can also be used to finish a dish and works well as a sweet and salty dipping sauce.

Place the light soy sauce and sugar in a small saucepan and gently simmer over a low heat. Stir until the sugar dissolves and then continue to simmer for about 5 minutes until the liquid starts to reduce and thicken.

Add the dark soy and sake, stir and leave to cool. Either use immediately or transfer to an airtight container and store in the fridge. It should keep for several weeks.

katsu curry sauce [2]

serves 2

2–3 tablespoons vegetable oil
1 onion, finely chopped
1 garlic clove, crushed
2.5cm piece of ginger, peeled
    and grated
1 teaspoon turmeric
2 heaped tablespoons mild
    curry powder
1 tablespoon plain flour
300ml Chicken or Vegetable
    Stock (*see* page 165 or 163)
100ml coconut milk
1 teaspoon light soy sauce
1 teaspoon caster sugar, to taste

An 'at home' take on our iconic curry sauce.

Place the oil in a saucepan over a medium heat. Add the onion, garlic and ginger and cook until softened. Lower the heat, add the spices and cook for 2–3 minutes.

Add the flour and stir over the heat to cook it out, then slowly add the chicken or vegetable stock. Bring to a simmer and add the coconut milk, soy sauce and sugar, to taste. For a perfectly smooth sauce, pass the mixture through a sieve.

Store in an airtight container in the fridge for up to 3 days.

 # gyoza sauce [3]

 vg

makes 175ml

1 small garlic clove, crushed
generous pinch of sea salt
½ red chilli, deseeded and
    finely chopped
50ml malt vinegar

1 tablespoon caster sugar
125ml light soy sauce
1 teaspoon sesame oil

A savoury and tart dipping sauce which pairs perfectly with our gyozas.

Place the garlic with the salt and chilli in a pestle and mortar and grind together until it forms a paste.

Transfer the paste to a saucepan with the vinegar and sugar and, over a low heat and stirring, simmer gently until the sugar dissolves. Stir in the soy sauce and sesame oil.

Either use immediately or transfer to an airtight container and store in the fridge. It should keep for several weeks.

spicy vinegar [4]

 vg

makes 150ml

50g caster sugar
2 tablespoons water
5 tablespoons malt vinegar
5 tablespoons light soy sauce
pinch of sea salt

½ red chilli, deseeded and
    finely chopped
3 coriander sprigs, stalks
    removed and leaves
    finely chopped

Spicy, sweet, sour and salty – typical flavours of South-east Asia. This makes a great dipping sauce or dressing.

Place the sugar and water in a small saucepan over a medium-low heat and stir until dissolved.

Remove from the heat and add the vinegar, soy sauce and a pinch of salt.

Store in an airtight container in the fridge for up to 4 weeks and stir in the chilli and coriander just before use.

feed your soul | wagamama

wagamama dressing [5]

makes 125ml

2 teaspoons finely chopped
  shallots
2.5cm piece of ginger, peeled
  and grated
1 garlic clove, crushed

1 ½ tablespoons rice wine vinegar
1 tablespoon tomato ketchup
1 tablespoon water
100ml vegetable oil
3 tablespoons light soy sauce

A true favourite which has stood the test of time.

Place all the ingredients in a bowl or large jar and whisk
together until smooth.

Store in an airtight container in the fridge for up to 3 days.

amai sauce [6]

makes 275ml

3 tablespoons caster sugar
1 tablespoon rice wine vinegar
1 tablespoon malt vinegar
1 ½ tablespoons tomato
  ketchup

2 tablespoons tamarind
  concentrate
1 tablespoon light soy sauce
1 tablespoon dark soy sauce
pinch of salt

**A sweet and sour dipping sauce, this works perfectly
in noodle stir-fry dishes or as a dipping sauce.**

Place the sugar and vinegars in a small saucepan over a
medium-low heat and stir until dissolved.

Add the tomato ketchup and tamarind and mix well, then
stir in the soy sauces and salt and bring back to the boil.
Using a wooden spoon, skim away any impurities that rise
to the surface. It might foam a little.

Reduce the heat and simmer for 30 minutes until it
becomes a sticky sauce.

tip | to make a tonkatsu style sauce, add 2 tablespoons
Worcestershire sauce, 1 crushed garlic clove and 1 teaspoon
finely sliced ginger.

yakitori sauce [7]

makes 125ml

1 tablespoon sake
1 tablespoon mirin
6 tablespoons light soy sauce
1 teaspoon sugar

A sweet Japanese marinade typically used to marinate proteins before grilling.

Place all the ingredients in a small saucepan and gently simmer over low heat until the sugar has dissolved and the sauce has reduced slightly. Set aside to cool.

 # firecracker sauce [8]

makes 250ml

50ml yakitori sauce (see left)
50ml oyster sauce or
   vegetarian oyster sauce
100ml sriracha sauce
2 tablespoons fish sauce or
   vegetarian oyster sauce

50ml vegetable oil
2 tablespoons dried chilli
   flakes, to taste
6 tablespoons runny honey or
   3 tablespoons agave syrup
   and 3 tablespoons sweet
   chilli sauce

Our signature sweet and fiery sauce, this can be used in stir-fry dishes and complements both protein and vegetable-based ingredients.

Place all the ingredients in a small saucepan over a medium-low heat, bring to the boil and then reduce the heat to a simmer.

Cook for about 15–20 minutes until the sauce thickens to a syrup-like consistency. Add more chilli flakes to taste.

Serve instantly or transfer to an airtight jar and keep in the fridge for up to 3 weeks.

thai green curry paste [9]

serves 8

4–6 medium green chillies, deseeded and roughly chopped
2 onions, roughly chopped
2 garlic cloves, crushed
2.5cm piece of ginger, peeled and chopped
2 lemongrass stalks, roughly chopped
zest and juice of 1 lime
small bunch of coriander
1 teaspoon ground cumin
1 teaspoon black peppercorns, crushed
2 teaspoons fish sauce
3 tablespoons vegetable oil
1 teaspoon sugar
generous pinch of sea salt

A fragrant green curry paste. Simply stir-fry to release the ingredients' oil and add coconut milk to create a rich Thai green curry.

Place all the ingredients in a food processor and blitz to a smooth paste.

Either use straight away or store in an airtight jar in the fridge for up to a week.

tip | to make this recipe vegetarian, replace the fish sauce with vegetarian oyster sauce.

chilli katsu sauce [10]   vg

makes 125ml

75ml sriracha sauce
50ml sweet chilli sauce
1 teaspoon paprika
2 teaspoons malt vinegar

A spicy, sweet and sour sauce, perfect for dipping or adding a sharp and spicy depth of flavour to dishes.

Place all the ingredients in a bowl or large jar and whisk together until smooth.

Store in an airtight container in the fridge for up to a month.

japanese pickles

pickling liquor

1 teaspoon coriander seeds

1 teaspoon cumin seeds

50ml water

juice of 1 lime

1–2 tablespoons caster sugar

1 teaspoon sea salt

vegetables

½ cucumber, finely sliced, seeds removed

50g daikon, finely sliced

50g salad radishes, finely sliced

100ml rice or white vinegar

This simple pickle recipe will make a difference to many meals, adding a spike of sharp flavour to cut through rich meat dishes or enhance a ramen or rice bowl.

Place a non-stick saucepan over a medium-low heat and, when hot, toast the coriander and cumin seeds for 1–2 minutes, being careful to ensure they don't burn.

Add all the remaining pickling liquor ingredients to the pan and, stirring, bring to a simmer. Once the sugar and salt have dissolved, remove the pan from the heat and set aside to cool.

Once cool, add the vegetables and leave to pickle for 10–30 minutes.

Store in an air tight, sterilised jar for up to a month.

kimchee

1 Chinese cabbage
2 carrots, peeled and cut into
   matchsticks or coarsely grated
60g coarse sea salt
½ daikon or 8 salad radishes,
   coarsely grated
4 spring onions, finely sliced

kimchee paste

3 garlic cloves, crushed
2.5cm piece of ginger, peeled and
   grated
2 tablespoons fish sauce or
   vegetarian oyster sauce
2 tablespoons gochujang or
   sriracha
1 tablespoon golden caster sugar
3 tablespoons rice vinegar

This classic Korean accompaniment is made by fermenting cabbage and carrots in a flavoursome sauce, pungent with garlic and spice. Kimchee adds flavour to many Asian dishes.

Slice the cabbage lengthways into four and remove the core from each piece. Place in a large bowl with the carrots and cover with the salt, ensuring the vegetables are well coated. Cover with water and set aside to brine for up to 2 hours.

To make the kimchee paste, place the garlic, ginger, fish sauce (if using), chilli paste, sugar and rice vinegar together in a small bowl and stir to blend.

Once the cabbage and carrot mixture is ready, drain and rinse under cold running water to remove any salt crystals.

Return the cabbage mixture to the large bowl and stir through the paste, along with the daikon and spring onions. Serve straight away or pack tightly into a large sterilised jar, seal and leave at room temperature to ferment overnight or for up to 72 hours.

While fermenting, insert a clean chopstick or butter knife every now and then to release any air bubbles. You can also add some additional brine to keep all the vegetables submerged if necessary.

A sealed jar of kimchee will keep in the fridge for up to 4 weeks. The flavour will improve the longer it's left.

tip | to make this recipe plant-based, replace the fish sauce with 1 tablespoon soy sauce and 1 tablespoon miso paste.

stocks

When it comes to ramen, it all starts with the broth. The broth is the foundation of the dish and is best when made from scratch, slowly simmered, needing little attention but without shortcuts. We understand that it's not always convenient to make your own stock and for ease and accessibility you can, of course, buy a ready-made substitute. We recommend a high-quality liquid version. There is, however, nothing quite like a ramen made with the real thing.

We have provided recipes for making a stock from scratch and we have also given the option of a quick stock, which can be made at the same time as cooking the rest of the dish.

vegetable stock

makes 1 litre

15 dried shiitake mushrooms
4 onions, peeled and roughly
    chopped
2 celery stalks, roughly chopped
4 carrots, peeled and roughly
    chopped
1 leek, roughly chopped
1 red chilli, deseeded and roughly
    chopped
2 garlic cloves, crushed
2.5cm piece of ginger, peeled
    and grated
2 thyme sprigs
6 sage leaves
pinch of sea salt
2 tablespoons tomato purée
1 tablespoon light soy sauce
pinch of caster sugar

Place the vegetables, chilli, garlic, ginger and herbs in a large stock pot and cover with 1¼ litres of water. Add a generous pinch of salt and bring to the boil.

Reduce the heat, cover and simmer for 30 minutes.

Strain the stock through a fine mesh sieve, discarding all the vegetables except the mushrooms.

Return the stock with the mushrooms to the pot, add the tomato purée and boil down the stock until it's reduced by a fifth.

Add the soy sauce and sugar and any more seasoning to taste.

Use immediately or store for up to 3–4 days in the fridge or up to 3 months in the freezer.

tip | if you're short on time, simply add the following ingredients to a pot, bring to the boil and leave to simmer for 10–15 minutes: 2 good quality stock cubes, 2 peeled and roughly chopped carrots, a few sprigs of flat leaf parsley, 2–3 litres of water and 2 leaves of Chinese leaf cabbage (optional).

beef stock

makes 1 litre

1kg beef bones (ask the butcher
   for these – rib and leg
   marrowbones work well)
1 heaped tablespoon tomato
   purée
1 large onion, roughly chopped
2 garlic cloves, crushed
2.5cm piece of ginger, peeled
   and grated
2 thyme sprigs
6 sage leaves
bunch of parsley
1 leek, roughly chopped
4 carrots, roughly chopped
2 celery sticks with tops left on,
   roughly chopped
4 tomatoes, roughly chopped
pinch of sea salt
1 teaspoon black peppercorns
pinch of caster sugar

Preheat the oven to 200°C, Gas Mark 6.

If your butcher hasn't prepared the bones, use a meat cleaver to chop them into smaller pieces.

Place the bones in a large roasting tin with the tomato purée, onion and garlic.

Cover the bones with water to a depth of about 2.5cm and roast for 40–45 minutes. Check occasionally and top up with more water if necessary.

Fill a large stock pot with 3 litres of water and bring to a simmer.

Add the roasted bones and all the browned bits from the roasting tin into the pot. Add the ginger, herbs, vegetables, salt and peppercorns to the pot and gently simmer for 4–6 hours, or longer if possible (the longer the cooking time, the stronger the flavour of the stock), topping up with water if it has evaporated. Skim away any foam that rises to the top.

Strain the liquid through a fine mesh sieve, then return it to the pot and simmer over a low heat until it has reduced by half, which will take at least an hour. Stir in a pinch of caster sugar.

Either use immediately or cool completely and store for up to 3 days in the fridge or up to 3 months in the freezer.

chicken stock

makes 1 litre

leftover bones and skin from
  a large cooked chicken
2 celery sticks with tops left on,
  roughly chopped
4 carrots, peeled and roughly
  chopped
1 leek, roughly chopped
4 onions, peeled and roughly
  chopped
2 garlic cloves, crushed
2.5cm piece of ginger, peeled
  and grated
2 thyme sprigs
6 sage leaves
bunch of parsley
1 teaspoon black peppercorns
generous pinch of sea salt
1 tablespoon light soy sauce
pinch of caster sugar

Place the leftover bones and skin from the chicken carcass into a large stock
pot and add the vegetables, onions, garlic, ginger, herbs and peppercorns.

Cover with 1½ litres of water, add a generous pinch of salt and bring to the boil
over a medium heat. Reduce to a simmer and partly cover.

Simmer for up to 4 hours, occasionally skimming away any foam that rises to the top.

Remove the bones and vegetables with a slotted spoon or spider ladle, and then
strain the stock through a fine mesh sieve. Discard all the vegetables.

If making the stock for future use, you may want to reduce the stock by cooking
it for a further hour or 2 so it becomes more concentrated and easier to store.

Add the soy sauce, caster sugar and any more seasoning to taste.

Either use immediately or cool completely and store for up to 3 days in the fridge
or up to 3 months in the freezer.

tip | if you're short on time, simply add 2 good quality chicken stock cubes, 500g
uncooked chicken thighs or wings, 1 chopped leek, 1 finely sliced carrot and 1 litre of
water to a pan and bring to a boil. Once boiling, leave to simmer for 30 minutes.

dashi

makes 1 litre

1 x 10cm piece of kombu
handful of dried bonito flakes

This light fish stock, which can be found in most large supermarkets,
is typically made from kombu; a combination of kelp seaweed and dried
bonito flakes. It is packed with deep umami flavour and adds great
depth and richness to stocks and broths.

Place the kombu with 1 litre of water in a stock pot over a medium heat.
Gently bring to the boil, then take off the heat and remove the kombu with
a slotted spoon.

Return the pot to the heat and add the bonito flakes. Turn up the heat and
simmer until almost at boiling point.

Take the pot off the heat and allow the bonito flakes to sink to the bottom.

Strain using a fine mesh sieve and either use immediately or freeze and use
within 3 months.

stock base

**makes 250g, enough for
approx. 8 ramen dishes**

2 tablespoons cornflour
150g duck fat
2 chicken stock cubes
1 tablespoon miso
1 tablespoon shiro dashi stock
   concentrate
1 tablespoon light soy sauce

This stock base is used in some of our ramen recipes to enrichen and
deepen the stock flavour. 'Shirodashi' is a white dashi liquid stock packed
with umami flavour from the dried bonito flakes used in its recipe.

First dilute the cornflour in a cup with 4 tablespoons cold water.

Meanwhile, place the duck fat in a small pot on a low heat. Add all the remaining
ingredients and gently whisk until smooth.

If not using immediately, place in an air tight container and leave to cool before
refrigerating. This will keep in the fridge for up to a month.

While our recipes have been designed to be simple to recreate, we have given the option of making pastry, pickles and more from scratch for those who would like to learn a new skill and master the art of creating a gyoza from scratch. We also know that unlike our restaurants, you will not likely have a teppan at home, so we have made sure these recipes will work in the most ordinary kitchen and so there is very little specific equipment that is required.

A wok is perhaps our most key piece of equipment but, if you do not own one, a non-stick frying pan works perfectly well. However, while we aren't too particular about what kind of equipment we use in our kitchens, we are passionate about the way we use it and take care of it. Therefore, if you do purchase a new wok, in our view it is essential that you 'season it' as this process will prevent rusting and ensure it lasts longer. The method is very simple; first, wash it in hot soapy water. Next, place the wok over a medium heat and burn it until the inside turns a deep blue colour. Once coloured, remove from the heat and coat with a layer of vegetable oil, ensuring the metal is thoroughly covered, and then leave this to soak in. Subsequently, after each use, wash and dry your wok thoroughly and then rub with a little oil as this will help prevent rusting and keep it in good condition.

We also use a teppan a lot for cooking our stir-fried noodle dishes and vegetables. This is a large, flat hot plate and so a heavy-bottomed non-stick frying pan makes a perfect substitute. In Japan, a bamboo steamer or 'seiro' is the preferred steaming vessel for buns, gyoza or dumplings. They are an inexpensive piece of equipment and can be found in most Asian supermarkets or high street kitchenware shops. However, a regular steamer will also work just fine.

The only other essential pieces of equipment are measuring spoons, kitchen scales, a measuring jug and a hand blender or food processor for making curry pastes, smoothies and juices. Deep bowls are perfect for serving ramen, but whatever bowls you have in your cupboard will work well. And finally, like in our restaurants, chopsticks are favoured.

hirata steamed buns

makes 18 buns

525g plain flour, plus extra for
    dusting
1½ tablespoons caster sugar, plus
    a pinch
½ teaspoon sea salt
1 teaspoon fast-action dried yeast
50ml milk
1 tablespoon sunflower oil, plus
    extra for brushing
1 tablespoon rice wine vinegar
1 teaspoon baking powder

Hirata are traditional Japanese steamed buns, otherwise known as 'bao' in China. They are delicious pillows of soft dough and, while they do take some time to prepare, are worth the effort. Fill with savoury fillings for an impressive side dish (*see recipes on page 144*).

Place the flour, sugar and salt in a large mixing bowl and stir to combine.

Dissolve the yeast with a pinch of sugar in 1 tablespoon of warm water, then add to the flour with the milk, sunflower oil, rice wine vinegar and 200ml tepid water. Using your hands, mix to form a dough, adding more tepid water if necessary.

Dust a clean work surface with flour and knead the dough for up to 15 minutes, until smooth, then place in a bowl and cover with a damp cloth. Set aside to rise until doubled in size – this can take up to 2 hours.

Once risen, tip the dough out onto a clean floured work surface and punch the centre. Using your hands, flatten out the dough and sprinkle with the baking powder, then knead for a final 5 minutes.

Using your hands, roll the dough into a long 3cm-thick sausage shape, then slice into 3cm-thick rounds, to make 18 rounds in total. Then roll each piece of dough into a ball and leave to rest for 3 minutes.

With a rolling pin, flatten each ball into an oval shape about 4mm thick.

Brush the surface of each oval of dough with a little oil, and also oil the length of a chopstick.

Place the chopstick in the centre of each oval of dough and fold the dough over the chopstick. Carefully slide away the oiled chopstick

Cut out 18 squares of parchment paper and arrange on a baking tray. Place a bun on each piece of paper, cover with lightly oiled clingfilm or a clean tea towel and set aside to prove in a warm place for around 1½ hours, until doubled in size.

Place a large steamer over a medium-high heat and steam the buns in batches for about 8 minutes, until risen and fluffy.

Prise open each bun and add a filling of your choice (see page 144). Eat while they're still warm.

tip | see recipe ideas for fillings on page 144.

feed your soul | **wagamama**

basic ramen noodles

250g all-purpose flour, plus extra
for dusting
pinch of sea salt
120ml water

While noodles are readily available in supermarkets, there is something very special about making your own from scratch. They are simple to make and this noodle recipe works perfectly for both ramen and stir-fry dishes.

Place the flour and salt in a large bowl and mix together. Using your hands or a spoon, keep stirring as you slowly pour in the water and, as soon as all the dry flour has been incorporated, stop adding water. Pat into a ball and place on a lightly floured surface.

Knead the dough until your hands are clean and the dough is smooth, about 10–15 minutes.

Place into a clean bowl and cover with a wet cloth. Set aside to rest for 30 minutes.

Transfer the dough to a clean floured work surface and roll out to flatten to an even thickness.

Keeping the rolling pin and the dough lightly floured to avoid any sticking, continue to roll out the dough into a 2mm-thick rectangle.

Fold over the dough lengthways (several times) to a width of around 5cm and, each time you fold, lightly dust the surface with flour. Trim away any irregular parts at the top and bottom if necessary, to create straight edges.

With a sharp (and dry) knife, slice the folded dough widthways into thin strips to make long ribbons. Dust a little flour onto the work surface before picking up and unspooling the noodles.

Unfold the noodles one by one, gently shaking off any excess flour.

Cook immediately in salted boiling water for 3–5 minutes. Store in the fridge for up to 3 days or allow to dry out for around 3 days, if using later.

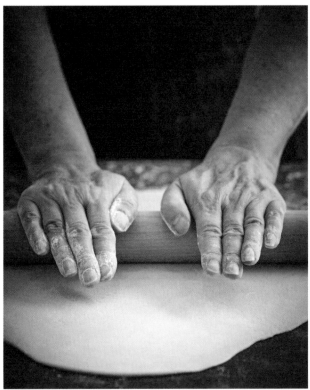

180g (1 cup) short grain or Thai
jasmine rice

perfect rice.
the wagamama way

Japanese cooking traditionally uses a short grain rice and cooks it in a way that gives it a glutinous, sticky texture. To prepare it perfectly, it is important that the ratio of rice to water is correct and, as a rule, this ratio is 2:3. We recommend a serving of 90g or ½ cup of rice per person (cups are far easier to use as a measure for rice).

Soak the rice in water for 30 minutes. Place the rice in a fine mesh sieve and leave to strain for at least 5 minutes to allow excess water to drain.

To cook, place 540ml water in a heavy-based saucepan, cover with a lid and bring to the boil. Once boiling, reduce the heat to the lowest setting, add the rice and leave to simmer for 10 minutes. It is important to leave the rice undisturbed during the entire cooking and resting process.

Take the pan off the heat and set aside with the lid still on for a further 10 minutes.

for basmati rice: add 180g (1 cup) basmati rice to a bowl and cover with water. Soak for 20 minutes, drain and rinse with water. Then add 2 cups of water to 1 cup of dry rice to the pan, set over a medium–high heat, bring to the boil and reduce to a simmer. Cover with a lid and cook for 10–12 minutes, remove lid and leave to stand for 5 minutes before serving.
for brown rice: add 180g (1 cup) brown rice to a bowl and cover with water. Soak for 20 minutes. drain and rinse with water. Then add 2 cups of water to 1 cup of dry rice to the pan, set over a medium–high heat, bring to the boil and reduce to a simmer. Cook for 30 minutes. Remove from the heat, cover with a lid and leave to stand for 5 minutes before serving.

150g tofu

perfectly pressed tofu

Tofu comes in many varieties, ranging from silken to extra firm. A firmer tofu is great for marinating and frying as it will keep its shape and texture. It is also perfect for a salad or curry. A medium or softer tofu is ideal for simmering in soups or coating in cornflour to fry off for a crispy texture.

To prepare, remove the tofu from the packet and place the block between 2 paper towels with a weight on top (a tin or book will do depending on the firmness of your tofu) for 10 minutes. Once the tofu has drained, it should feel a little firmer. Slice into even cubes.

Based on your recipe, you may want to coat and fry your tofu pieces. To do this, prepare a shallow bowl of cornflour and coat each piece of tofu well. Heat 2 tablespoons of vegetable oil in a frying pan or wok on a medium heat. Once hot add the tofu and fry, turning occasionally until crispy and golden brown. Place the cooked tofu onto a paper towel covered plate to drain excess oil until needed.

gyoza skins

makes 35–40 skins

240g strong white flour, plus extra
for dusting
½ teaspoon salt
120ml water, just boiled
cornflour, for dusting
3 tablespoons vegetable oil

Ready-made gyoza skins are available in most Asian supermarkets, but why not have a go at making your own from scratch, (*see* page 129 for filling recipes). The process is mindful and rewarding.

Sift the flour into a large mixing bowl. In another bowl, add the salt to the just-boiled water and mix until dissolved.

Add the salt water to the flour, little by little, stirring with chopsticks or a spatula as you go. Once the flour and water have started to combine, form the dough into a ball with your hands. If too dry, add an extra ½ tablespoon of water at a time.

Transfer the dough to a floured work surface and knead for up to 10 minutes until the texture is smooth and elastic.

Cut the dough ball in half and roll each piece into a log, approximately 4cm in diameter. Wrap each log in clingfilm and set aside to rest for 30 minutes.

Once rested, unwrap the dough, sprinkle some cornflour onto your work surface and slice each log into approximately 12 pieces. Arrange these on a large plate and cover with a clean damp tea towel to prevent the dough from drying out.

Using your hands, roll each piece of dough into a ball and then press flat. Next, using a rolling pin, roll the dough (turning 90 degrees after every roll) to create a thin, round circle that is approximately 8–9cm in diameter.

Using an 8cm cookie cutter, press down onto the dough to cut out a perfect circle, then transfer to a plate and dust lightly with cornflour to prevent the skins from sticking together as they accumulate. Re-roll the scraps to create additional skins. Cover the wrappers with damp kitchen towel whilst making the gyozas. Or, if not using immediately, cover with cling film and keep in the fridge for 3–4 days, or in the freezer for up to a month.

When you are ready to fill the gyoza, take a heaped teaspoon of filling and place it in the centre of each piece of dough. Fold one side over to encase the filling and bring the edges together, pinching them to seal. Finally, pleat the edges together.

Heat 2 tablespoons of the oil in a large non-stick frying pan. Once hot, working in batches so as not to overcrowd the pan, add the gyozas and cook for 3–4 minutes until the underside turns golden brown.

Once browned, add 60ml water to the pan and cover with a lid. Steam for 3 minutes, then remove the lid and cook off the excess water. Add the remaining oil and continue to cook until each gyzoa has crisped and turned brown. Once completely cooked, plate immediately and serve with our gyoza dipping sauce (see page 150).

index

feed your soul | **wagamama**

acknowledgements

There are many people wagamama would like to thank for this book, including: Emma Woods, our CEO who not only continues to inspire and lead us but also commissioned this project. Steve Mangleshot, our Executive Chef, whose passion and love of Asia has ensured that wagamama food is loved all over the world. Andre Johnstone, our Marketing Director, for driving the project forward and for his creative involvement throughout. Jasmin Ayling, our Head of Food Innovation, who had a vision and stuck to it: she led the creation of the cookbook, including direction of the design and food photography and has taken each wagamama recipe and written it so that anyone can cook these recipes at home. Helen Hyland, our Brand Manager, who has told our story, shared knowledge and showcased our beliefs throughout.

And to everyone else involved in this project, including Surendra Yejju, Sarah Langley, Sita Dobbs and Karl Thompson for all of their hard work and input. Howard Shooter, Denise Smart, Paul Palmer-Edwards and the Kyle Books team, including Joanna Copestick, Judith Hannam and Isabel Gonzalez for bringing the book to life.

A big thank you to all of our teams here at wagamama; our Front and Back of House teams for delivering the wagamama magic and our central support team at 'noodle HQ', for being the engine behind the brand.

But, of course, the wagamama experience would not be the same without our hardworking chefs who bring our dishes to life each day, so a special thanks to all of our Chefs.

As special recognition, we have dedicated the following page to our Development Chefs, National Training Chefs, Senior Head Chefs and Head Chefs:

Abbe Adou
Adam Kochelka
Adam Pietrzak
Adolfo Rodrigues
Alexander Silva
Alistair Ross
Alwyn Lobo
Andy Ariyanayagam
Anna Rapala
Anwar Bawady
Ardhendu Bandyopadhyay
Arron French
Arvind Rawat
Ashley Kay
Bal Limbu
Balaji Meedur
Bernard Lis
Bhaskar Ramaswamy
Blahima Diarassouba
Brett Holwill
Carmelo Botto
Chafik Saidoun
Charles Spinney
Charlotte Staples

Christopher Gideon
Constanta Chirazic Lupu
Craig McBea
Curtis Taylor
Damian Lukaszewski
Daniel Mackenzie
Daniel Szavai
Dariusz Czubak
Dariusz Majewski
Daryl Grant
David McKenzie
Davide Perna
Dawid Urbanski
Denis Christie
Dinesh Balasubramanian
Eduart Mjeshtre
Elaine Josefa De Andrade
Emma Gutteridge
Fabricio Pereira
Francis Walsh
Ganessen Appavoo
Georgios Maletsikas
Grzegorz Gabryjolek
Grzegorz Mikolajczuk
Harmik Suri
Henry Mugridge
Henry Staple
Ictiandro De Azevedo Alexandre
Imran Parchment
Jacek Mercik
Jake Manton

Jakub Rozworowski
James McMahon
Jamie Henderson
Jamie Windle
Janusz Wlosianski
Jay Bryant
Jessica Marsh
Jesus Carreon Mosqueda
Jesus Jaramillo Gil
Joanna Zolyniak-Swierk
Junior Lopes
Kamel Bahloul
Karl Varney
Katarzyna Pachuta
Kevin Reeder
Kieren Wilson
Koray Akbulut
Krishan Sharma
Krystian Boratynski
Krzysztof Zborowski
Kuldeep Rathore
Kunal Barve
Madhusudhanan
   Soundararajan
Mahdi Berkani
Manish Singh
Marcin Gosztkowski
Marek Kliber
Marek Puscikowski
Marek Szuszkiewicz
Mariusz Zuk
Marzena Szydlowska

Michal Alichniewicz
Michal Galica
Miguel Rocha
Mounir Khadraoui
Musendeka Kibassa-maliba
Muthu Krishnan
Nabish Rai
Omar Dem
Pankaj Kumar
Paul Dixon
Phil Clyde
Piotr Zielinski
Prasenjeet Chakraborty
Pritam Majumder
Priti Ingle
Przemyslaw Zielinski
Puneet Bhoocher
Radoslaw Skora
Rafael Pedrosa Borja
Rafal Proracki
Raghavendra Chetty
Reda Nouar
Ricardo Pais Abal
Riccardo Seffer
Richard Hamilton
Rolands Kirsteins
Rosa Maria Honorio
   De Almeida
Sameer Khadpe
Sean Lockwood
Seby Mascarenhas
Sergei Versuta

Shereif Elfahham
Sherif Ibrahim
Shiwen Wang
Sivachandran Balakumar
Stefan Townsend
Sunil Shetty
Sunny Obakpolor
Tathagata Mandal
Theophile Adissa
Tiju Thomas
Tim Hunt
Tomasz Kuszneruk
Tomasz Ptasinski
Urszula Przybylska
Victor Laskary
Vihangkumar Patel
Vincenzo Priolo
Warren Cruickshank
William Baird
Wojciech Wozny
Xhezair Kasamaj
Yasmine Omitade
Yogesh Mantri
Zacharias Gamvrillis